For:

A Man in Moccasins

We have never met, yet your kindness shines through your words and deeds.

Thank you so much for sending the cards of 'The Chief' please accept this book in return.

Regards, Ruari

RUARI MACLEAN July 2020

The right of Ruari Maclean to be identified as the
Author of the Work has been asserted by him in accordance
with the Copyright, Designs and Patents Act 1988.

A Man in Moccasins © Ruari Maclean 2020

Editor: Shaun Russell & Will Rees
Cover: Leanne Jones, leannejones.co.uk

Printed and bound in the UK by
Severn, Bristol Road, Gloucester, GL2 5EU

ISBN: 978-1-913637-01-9

Published by
Candy Jar Books
Mackintosh House
136 Newport Road, Cardiff, CF24 1DJ, Wales, UK
www.candyjarbooks.co.uk

All rights reserved.
No part of this publication may be reproduced, stored in a
retrieval system, or transmitted at any time or by any means,
electronic, mechanical, photocopying, recording or otherwise
without the prior permission of the copyright holder. This
book is sold subject to the condition that it shall not by way of
trade or otherwise be circulated without the publisher's prior
consent in any form of binding or cover other
than that in which it is published.

Dedication

This book is dedicated to the memory of John Duart Willard Maclean (1931-2017), otherwise known within the South Wales community in which he played a very active part as 'Johnny Mac'. At various times he was:

High Sheriff for West Glamorgan – a role that promotes the voluntary sector within the community; coach, chairman and later president of Llanelli Scarlets Rugby Football Club; former player and president of Swansea Uplands RFC; former player for Mumbles Cricket Club; president of Pontarddulais Cricket Club; president of Pontarddulais Town Band – one of the most successful brass bands in Britain; president of Côr Glandulais, a mixed choir; liveryman of the Worshipful Company of Tinplate Workers; officer in the Royal Welch Fusiliers, who fought in the Korean War; church warden at St Michaels' Church in Wales, Golden Grove.

All of these associations gave John a rich appreciation of his Celtic life, but he was equally proud of his Canadian dad, American grandmother, Scottish grandfather and adopted indigenous uncle, who all added to the cultural mix of his heritage.

A Man in Moccasins is one of his legacies, and a tribute to a man who embraced diversity in society.

Foreword

This is an incredible story. I first heard it in 1992 when I was playing for the Barbarians, one of the most famous rugby clubs in the world. The victorious side that toured South Wales included a future World Cup winning skipper in Martin Johnson, and was captained by Ruari. He introduced me to his uncle, a former Llanelli Scarlets coach, who wanted to make known his family ties with Canada. It's taken nearly thirty years to get a remarkable tale into print. It has been well worth the wait....

Glenn Ennis

Ex Canada rugby captain, current stunt coordinator and stuntman, actor, writer and producer in TV and film.

Preface

The following is a dramatisation of a true story. The lives of John and Annie Maclean have been researched through a variety of sources listed at the end of the text, and it is around this framework that a narrative has been constructed.

It could not have been written without the endeavours of my uncle JDW (John) Maclean, his wife Ann, and the full support of their children Emma and Alex. Their collection of letters, journal extracts and family papers have enabled this personal interpretation of events to be written.

Chapter One

*'I stand outside the Tavern Door
My dad's in there upon the floor.
Wouldn't it be really sweet
If he were here upon his feet.'*

…sang the thirteen year old apprentice shoemaker as he waited patiently for his father to send out patrons on a dreich Glasgow evening. The brisker the trade, however, the drunker Old John became. Customers would occasionally drop the odd ha'penny in Young John's tin cup as he sang, and leave him their copy of *The Tilly*, a maritime newspaper, for him to read at home. Little did he realise that the next thirty-six hours would frame his life.

The following afternoon, his mother, Alice, read snippets of *The Tilly* aloud as she cooked, becoming increasingly agitated, like the broth swirling in the big pot in front of her.

'Can you believe it?' she shouted, defiantly waving *the Tilly* above the stove. She looked like she was trying to shake the words from the newspaper into the soup, so that her family could digest them. The four brothers waited patiently for their bellies to be filled, whilst their dad, a talented boot closer, sat in his chair in the corner of the room, cleaning his pipe, ready for a smoke before the evening meal. Old John would travel anywhere to find work, but he preferred to work from home on benches in his basement, with his family. Alice had been a sewing teacher at Burgh Academy, and she used those skills to be the bootbinder. Their sons had been apprenticed from the age of six. Handmade shoes were stitched in a particular order, with the last and closing seam being the most important one.

'Son,' Alice continued, 'read the section "News from the Americas", please.'

Young John stood next to his mother with *the Tilly* in his hand. His mother tapped his broad shoulders, encouraging him to pull them back and stand up straight and true to deliver his words.

Young John was never irritated by his mother's fine eye for detail. She was always so positive, and did things with such good grace that you couldn't possibly get annoyed. Lovingly Alice put one finger on her son's chiselled chin, lightly raising it so that he spoke up and out to the room and not down to the floor.

'All of you listen,' ordered Alice, and her son began to read.

'May 22nd, 1856 – Congressman Preston Brooks of South Carolina beat Senator Charles Sumner with a cane in the hall of the United States Senate for a speech Sumner had made attacking southerners who supported slavery.

'May 24th, 1856 – The Pottawatomic Massacre

occurred, a group of followers of the radical abolitionist John Brown killing five white homesteaders in Franklin County, Kansas.

'March 3rd, 1857 – The day dubbed "The Weeping Time" in Savannah, Georgia, on which Pierce Butler sold four hundred and thirty-six black men, women and children from horse boxes.

'March 6th, 1857 – The Supreme Court ruled that slaves are not citizens and so cannot sue for freedom, driving the country further towards civil war.'

'A civil war in America,' Alice interjected, 'fought between those in favour of slavery and those against it. I pray those fighting for the good of all humanity prevail.'

Young John nodded. He had his father's physical presence and good looks, but the backbone of his mother. He had taken the best attributes of each of his parents, melding them into a single whole – a human spirit that was reflective, with a strong conscience and the overwhelming desire to make his mark in the world.

Alice dished the soup out, breaking stale bread amongst the bowls to try and supplement the meagreness of the meal she had prepared. Her husband placed his pipe on the sideboard and joined them at the table.

'Let us eat,' said Alice. Attempting to stimulate discussion, she returned to the subject of America.

'Slavery is inhumane. But the massacre at Pottawatomic, when abolitionists killed white slavers, shows that you can't fight fire with fire. It only stokes a bigger conflagration, and still more deaths. The strength of your words and the power of your argument must be backed up by positive actions. That is the best way to affect change.'

Her son listened to every word she spoke. What neither of them knew, because in 1864 news took so long to filter through, was the Civil War that had started in 1861 was to all intents and purposes over. The Thirteenth Amendment abolishing slavery had been ratified by the Senate on April 8th, 1864, although it wouldn't be made law until the following year.

Everyone had to help clearing the table. It was the time of day Young John liked least. Soon he would go off with his dad to the pubs to work. Alice would remind Old John about his drinking, and he would see this as interference. The conviviality of dinner would be soured by their mutual resentment.

But as it happened, on this particular evening his father meekly accepted Alice's warning. The truth was, Old John was worried: Alice's coughing, which had been ever present since typhoid had struck the area, was worsening. He offered not to go to work that evening, and it was only when he turned away that Young John saw the fear in his eyes.

All of a sudden, Alice doubled up in front of her family, churning up mouthfuls of blood onto the floor. Old John acted swiftly, barking instructions to his eldest to fetch the doctor; meanwhile his younger sons were waved upstairs, and Hamish instructed to look after them.

They obeyed instantly. The seriousness of the situation was felt by them all. Old John held his wife in his strong arms, trying to comfort her. In a while the doctor appeared, by which time Alice was in bed. Young

John wanted to stay with his mum, but was ushered away by his dad and told to help Hamish with his younger brothers.

Young John did what he was told, trying to keep everyone's spirits up by recounting stories their mother had told them when they were young. All the time they could hear more retching from below. They prayed it was soup coming up, not more blood.

Eventually, the youngest fell asleep, and Young John crept outside his parent's bedroom door, where he could faintly hear the muffled voices of his dad and the good doctor.

The medic was hoping that the suspected intestinal bleeding might slow, allowing Alice to last the night. Then it would be a case of trying to get her to Glasgow Royal Infirmary. A new surgical block had been opened a few years back, overseen by the professor of surgery, Joseph Lister, who was pioneering new techniques in anti-sepsis, resulting in much lower mortality rates. If they could operate on Alice, they might have a chance of saving her.

Hearing footsteps on the floorboards inside the room, Young John felt a lump in his throat. His dad opened the door to find his son standing there; both had tears in their eyes.

'Make a pot of tea, will you, son. Your mother has made a request. Can you fetch the Reverend William Cullum? Ask him to bring a hymn book too.'

'Aye, dad. I will.'

Young John made some tea, took it to his father, and went off on his errand to find the amiable minister, who ran the Sunday Church School that all the boys attended twice a month, and where Alice volunteered.

Once they returned, Young John checked on his brothers and then sat waiting at the table downstairs, where only hours earlier his mother had been eating and talking so vividly. He drifted in and out of sleep before he was gently shaken awake by his father.

'Your mother would like to see you. Are you up to it? It is not a pleasant room to be in.'

Young John nodded sorrowfully.

'If you can, will you sing her "Jesus, Lover of my Soul"? She'll understand if you can't, but it will bring her comfort.'

Young John summoned up all his courage and went up to where his mother lay. He entered the most sombre of rooms, carrying a small candle, but fortified by a conviction to carry out his task. It felt like the hardest thing he had ever had to do. Dr Wyllie and the Reverend William Cullum tried to encourage the young lad with gentle smiles, and the latter passed him the *Wesleyan Hymn Book*.

Alice looked at her son with such affection. Her husband squeezed in to the small bedroom, trying to be as unobtrusive as he could be. Young John took one deep breath before he started singing.

Unusually he struggled to find the right pitch, and to his audience it sounded as though he was faltering. Young John, however, sensed a physical change in his voice: it was undeniably starting to break.

As Young John finished his heart wrenching rendition, he fought the urge to cry. He felt he had to control his emotions. He had gauged the mood in the room, and he had guessed that this was likely to be the last thing he ever did for his mother.

Alice limply beckoned her son forward. He knelt by her side on the blood-splattered floorboards, and she ruffled his hair, as she did so often. He leaned close to hear her words as she whispered to him

'It is all right to cry, you know. Too many men are too weak to cry.' She paused to gather her breath.

'I want you to promise me that you will be honest with your feelings. That you will weep when your soul needs an outlet and that you will lay your conscience bare to those you are with. They will appreciate your honesty, and it will empower you.'

John nodded, and Alice said a prayer, cupping her hand on his strong cheekbone. He shed tears that fell into her hand, and he saw her fingers flinch as the droplets gathered in her creased palm to form rivulets that ran down her arm and onto the bed sheet.

As he wept he looked at his mother, and her emaciated face broke into a faint smile. She said a few more words. Then her hand fell to the bed. She was gone.

As the sun rose it dawned on John that his father would not be able to cope without their mother's steadying influence, and that it was he who would effectively become responsible for the household.

'Never shall I forget the day she left us for the better land. I was knelt by her side as she spoke in my ear, "O happy day when Jesus washed my sins away". A few minutes later she was gone. I know that my school books will be packed up in a trunk and my life will be full of darkness, for my best friend on earth has left me.'

John's days were spent in work and his nights in

study. He shared his grief with his journal and lost himself in learning. He borrowed a school book, *Smiths Principia Latina*, from a friend and memorised the Latin as he sat on his shoemaker's seat. It was there that he studied Greek, too.

'I resolve to give up my companions and pleasures and will study with enthusiasm however I can. Every penny I save will go towards books, and every spare minute I will spend on study.'

Hamish and John shared duties with their father in the evening rounds of the pubs, and during that time they begged for candle ends, which they would stuff in their pockets so that John could fashion some sort of illumination by which to work.

When Hamish and his father were out at work and his brothers Andrew and Scott were tucked up in bed, John found solace in the quietness of study. As long as the candles lasted, he had time to himself.

He was inspired by the stories he heard at Sunday School. It was the heyday of Christian foreign missions, and John loved to hear stories of their work in Fiji and Japan. It all seemed so far away from his life in Dumbarton, and he dreamt one day he would join their cause.

He set about assiduously developing the skills required for missionary work:

'I accustomed myself to see how long I could do without sleep. I began to try and see how many nights I could do without it. For three months I was only four times in bed. When I tired, the candle was blown out and my head laid on the table or held in my hands.

'In fifteen to twenty minutes I would wake shivering

with cold, light my candle and study again. During the day I left off using butter and putting sugar in my tea, wore no underclothing and did without socks.'

Then, joy of joys, gas street lighting came to his road. Muirkirk, some 50 miles south, had in 1859 become the first British town to have street lighting, and the technology had steadily spread from there. Now when it got dark John could position his desk by a front window and not be reliant on candles. It felt like the ultimate luxury.

As the sons advanced through their teens they became increasingly independent. They had to, just to survive.

'I shall ever carry with me the bitter knowledge of what I suffer without my mother. There are times when I stand in the snow after midnight begging for something to eat or drink and having no money to pay for it as my father lies at home wild with delirium tremens [chronic alcoholism].'

The weight of responsibility was a heavy burden for John. He occupied himself with 'furious study' and went to the Methodist Church in town on a regular basis for the better part of a decade. It was there that the Reverend William Cullum became his mentor until he left for a post in England; however, the two continued to keep in touch. It was the reverend who John still looked to for paternal sanction.

John had written to Reverend Cullum to tell him of his intention to sit the entrance exam of the University of Glasgow in October 1873. The reverend replied that he was travelling back up to Scotland in late September to renew old acquaintances. He invited John to hear him give a sermon on Sunday 27th September, after which tea and sandwiches would give them ample opportunity to talk about the future.

Reverend William Cullum now lived in Portsmouth, where his brother was a wealthy merchant. The reverend's nephew, the merchant's son, was a similar type of character to John: a Methodist with drive and a keenness to travel. He, however, had the funding to realise his dreams.

His father had business links in Toronto and contacts with the Methodist Church of Canada. He had arranged for his son's passage by steamship to Quebec, where initially he would stay with a family and be apprenticed to a carpenter so that he could earn his keep while waiting for opportunities to arise with the local church. Everything was arranged and the steam ticket was booked for October 20th, 1873.

But Cullum's nephew was a keen horseman, and unfortunately, in early September, he had been involved in a serious accident, having been thrown from his horse in a point-to-point race. He was lucky to come away alive, but he would require further treatment if he were ever to walk again. Cullum was there to offer John his nephew's ticket.

As the reverend ran through the arrangements later that afternoon, John came up with a litany of reasons why he could not go. As he reeled them off, Hamish, who had accompanied his brother, couldn't help laughing.

John frowned at his younger sibling. 'I'm standing here exasperated, and all you can do is look at me all *fou rire*. Why the giggles, Hamish?'

'Since Mum died,' his brother replied, 'you have dedicated yourself to looking after us. Dad couldn't, but you have. Will you just listen to yourself, John? You're trying to find every reason under the sun not to go, when you know as well as I do this is too good an opportunity to miss. Not only have you every right to take this chance, you deserve it. The University of Glasgow can wait. You know I am more than capable in the workshop, and so are Andrew and Scott. Mum would have wanted you to seize the moment. Go out there, work, study, immerse yourself in the church and shape your future. I'd never have believed it, but this is divine providence.'

The reverend assured John that his brother had paid for the ticket out of a sense of philanthropy, that he saw the young man as someone who deserved good fortune, and that he knew John would not abuse the faith shown in him. His brother would not countenance any remuneration; all that he required were twice yearly letters keeping him abreast of developments.

John was told to keep the small amount of savings he had; he would need them to live on once he arrived in Canada. Eventually he was persuaded. Deep down, he had known since the reverend had first made his case that this was the opportunity he had been waiting for.

He had only a few days to organise all he needed before travelling down to the south coast of England with the reverend. The long journey from Glasgow to Portsmouth gave plenty of time for William and John to talk about the challenges the young man would face. John would be under the direction of the chairman of the Methodist Church of Canada. There would be no formal contract, his employment beginning with a probationary period where each could observe the other to see if there was a mutual future. If John showed an aptitude for preaching, he might ultimately be taken on as a lay preacher, but first he would have to demonstrate his worth.

So it was with trepidation, but also a huge feeling of excitement, that on October 20th, 1873, John boarded the steamer that was to start the journey of a lifetime.

Chapter Two

She was born in Buffalo, New York in early 1857, and christened Sarah Anne, but to her parents, Richard and Susannah Barker, she was never known as anything other than Annie.

The couple had married in Yorkshire, England, in 1850 and emigrated a year later. They were young, energetic and excited to create a new life for themselves in the Land of the Free. But as as soon as Annie, their last of four daughters, had arrived, they moved to Guelph, Canada, just forty-three miles (seventy kilometres) from Toronto, because of Richard's increasing business there.

However, Richard found himself back across the border as soon as April 1861. Like many other Methodists, he felt that Lincoln's presidential victory in 1860 heralded the arrival of the kingdom of God in America. Despite having four young children, he enlisted on Lincoln's side in the American Civil War.

Richard returned home four years later to immerse himself in his family, his work and his church. On July 1st 1867, the Dominion of Canada was proclaimed, with

John A Macdonald, another Glaswegian, as its first prime minister.

Annie and her sisters flourished under Susannah's tutelage. They were bright, independent girls with forceful characters, who successively graduated from the Wesleyan Female College with far more interest in pursuing their studies than in finding a husband.

Annie loved helping children to achieve their best, and as in turn she graduated from college, she felt she would see the summer out then seek a full time posting in a local school as a teacher. Her mother and father agreed with her plan – but as they got ready for church on a Sunday in June, 1875, little did they know that everything was about to change.

Richard crabbed awkwardly down the pew, closely followed by Susannah and their four daughters, Olive, Heather, Doris and Annie. The daughters always sat by age, with Olive next to Susannah, and Annie at the end of the pew. It was about the only tradition the Barker girls didn't question. It was just the way it was.

Into the midst of such cordiality strode a strikingly handsome young lay preacher. He was met by smiles of encouragement and murmurs of approval from the four eligible young ladies sitting in the second row.

John Maclean had prepared assiduously for his first sermon, going through it time and time again. No-one could have done more to earn this opportunity. He had completely restructured the Sunday School at Vienna Church, where he worshipped. His approach was to keep preaching to a minimum; it was all about engagement and activity.

He reached the pulpit, his small Bible and hymnbook in one hand and some notes in the other. It was a warm summer's day, and the doors front and back were open to allow a breeze to cool the congregation. He welcomed everyone warmly, looking to the back of the church so that his voice would project to those sitting furthermost from him. He looked back down to his aide memoire, which had been sitting on top of his hymn book. It had gone! His heart jumped. A gust had blown the paper into the audience.

A young woman grabbed it and rose to return it, and as John lowered his gaze to thank her, his eyes were met by the most beautiful vision of loveliness he had ever seen. Annie was transfixed too. Flustered, John played for time as he tried to gather himself. Annie had completely knocked him off his stride. He was out of kilter and he knew it. The audience sensed his nervousness as he wedged his notes between Bible and hymnbook and started again.

He had a sonorous voice which filled the church. He told of a company of old soldiers from the Union and Confederate armies who, post American Civil War, were reconciled and at peace with one another.

A former Confederate was telling the group how he had been detailed one night to shoot a certain exposed sentry of the opposing army. The Confederate soldier crept nearer and nearer and was about to fire from point blank range when the sentry began to sing 'Jesus, Lover of my Soul'.

As the oblivious Union soldier came to the words 'Cover my defenceless head/With the shadow of Thy wing', the hidden Confederate lowered his gun and stole away back to his troops. 'I can't kill that man,' he said, 'even if he were ten times my enemy.'

In the company of soldiers sharing their war stories was an old Union soldier, who asked, 'Was that in the Atlanta campaign of '64?'

'Yes.'

'Then I was the Union sentry!'

And he went on to tell how, on that night, knowing the danger of his post, he had been greatly depressed, so to keep up his courage he had begun to hum the hymn and sing the verses he knew. By the time he had finished, he was entirely calm, even fearless. Through the song, John told his audience, God had spoken to two souls.

Throughout the sermon John's concentration was such that he was oblivious to what had been going on in the second row. His inexperience of preaching and the pressure of the occasion had got to him, but he was unaware of how his nervousness had manifested itself. John's broad Glaswegian accent, which had mellowed in the time he'd been in Canada, had come back with a passion.

Olive, the mischief maker of the family, could hardly understand a word the young preacher was saying. Slowly, she tilted her head forward and looked down the line of her sisters. Inexorably, Annie was drawn to her eldest sister's gaze; though she knew she shouldn't look towards her, she couldn't help it.

Olive pulled a face as though she'd just eaten a handful of sour blueberries, at the same time pointing at her ear as if to say, 'What is this preacher talking about?'

Her mother tapped Olive's hand down but it was too

late. Olive knew the effect she would have on Annie, the profligate giggler of the family. No matter how hard she tried to suppress the mirth in the pit of her tummy, it gathered in force and spread like a virus over her whole body.

Within seconds the Barker pew was rocking with the rhythm of quaking bodies and silent laughter. All the daughters were infected. Their heads all bowed, every sister tried to gain control of something that had a force all of its own.

Their father tried to instil some sobriety to proceedings, giving them his iciest stare whenever he could catch their eyes. But this only fanned the flames.

This émigré preacher deserved a chance, and Richard Barker, a Yorkshireman who had arrived with a gruff accent of his own, wanted his daughters to show more civility.

But as much as Annie longed to listen to John, she was undone by her sister's abilities to press her buttons. John had a mellifluous voice that was highlighted when he pronounced his *r*s. The tip of his tongue vibrated against the top of his palate, making the *r* roll along poetically.

Doris, sitting next to Annie, purred like a cat in imitation, which set Annie off again. She pretended to cough to cover the quivering mass of bones that she had become. But she knew it was hopeless. Gathering her dress up, she swept down the aisle and out into fresh air to try and compose herself.

This quelled the commotion, and in a few minutes Annie was safe to return and hear the end of John's sermon. At its conclusion he opened his hymn book, smoothed the pages and began to sing the song that the Union soldier had sung, a song that meant so much to John, 'Jesus, Lover of My Soul'.

Since singing it to his mother on her death bed, he had been in many congregations that had risen for this hymn, but he had merely mouthed the words. Today he kept himself in check in the early verses, but as he thought back to that most desperate of nights, he invested in the hymn a part of him that had not yet been released.

After the sermon, Richard approached John to congratulate him on such a powerful delivery, and to apologise for his daughters' lack of savoir faire. Richard Barker assumed full responsibility for their misdemeanours, and by way of recompense, he invited the young preacher to Sunday lunch the next time he appeared on the circuit, in a month's time. John assured him that he had been so caught up in his first sermon he was unaware of what Richard was talking about.

The young preacher then stayed to help out at Sunday School, where Annie volunteered. She was captivated by his contribution, and the time flew by before he bade her a fond farewell.

The young Scot was the main topic of conversation when the family ate lunch, with the youngest sister regaling everyone with his positive qualities.

'He got to know everyone's name so quickly,' Annie said, 'and he really listened when people spoke. He gave them time and demanded others did too. He got the children playing games. He was strict but he had a sense of fun and he was so encouraging! Oh! He will make such a good—'

'Husband!' Olive interjected, and the family all squealed with delight.

'I was going to say "Minister",' said Annie defensively. But then she gave up any pretence of indifference. 'Is it that obvious?' They all nodded.

'Do you think he likes me?'

'Well, we can judge that when he comes to lunch in four weeks time,' said their father

Annie couldn't contain her excitement. 'He's coming to lunch!'

Chapter Three

Susannah never let their good-sized house be anything other than spick and span, but for the young preacher's lunch visit, Annie helped her mum dust and polish everywhere so that every room gleamed.

In the week, Richard had announced that after the lunch he would give John some voice coaching. He'd wished somebody had taken the time to help him when he had first set foot in North America. He recognised John's oratorical skills, but could discern that the young man needed to soften his vowel sounds, and avoid exaggerating his rhotic consonants, rolling his *r*s' and distracting his audience.

Annie was secretly disappointed. She had imagined going for a walk with John, maybe showing him around the garden. Never mind, she thought, she would look forward to the day regardless.

When Sunday finally came around, such was Annie's excitement, she couldn't eat her eggs in the morning. After breakfast, all the daughters helped each other brush and plait their hair. They promised their father they would not, under any circumstances, fall into the merriment that had nearly wrecked John's inaugural sermon.

They were true to their word, and the service went off without interruption. John could not match the emotional pitch of his first outing, but he spoke well and with greater clarity. In the interim he had also been able to preach at Vienna Church, and he was becoming more accomplished with every sermon.

He, too, was a little nervous about lunching with the Barkers. After the service, everyone stood outside the church exchanging pleasantries and enjoying the warmth of the sun on their faces, other than those with parasols who preferred the shade. Richard introduced his family, and Annie desperately tried not to stare.

There was then the rigmarole of who was to walk with whom on the way back to the house. Nobody had really thought this through, and the sisters immediately manoeuvred to get Annie next to John. In the confusion, she caught her shoe in her dress and nearly fell. Just in time, Olive grabbed Annie's arm, tucked it under hers and set off, declaring, 'We'll lead. John, please walk with my mother. Father, can you bring up the rear?'

Richard nodded and smiled. Olive was a strong character, much like him in many ways, and she would undoubtedly make someone a wonderful wife one day, if that was what she wanted. He had no doubt in his mind it would be her that decided who, when or whether she would marry.

As they entered the house, Susannah issued a set of instructions – although of course, everyone had already been briefed as to what was expected of them. In the flurry of activity, Richard invited John into the library.

'Best keep to ourselves for half-an-hour, John, otherwise we'll be in the way.'

As he followed his host, John marvelled at the homely feel of the room. There were books on architecture, many on engineering and plenty of novels too. Doris brought in a jug of lemonade and two glasses and made herself scarce.

'Fortunately, John, all my daughters like to read. It is so important, don't you think?'

'It is one of my greatest pleasures.'

John perused the shelves until, turning from some leather clad editions, he came to a gilt framed picture hanging on the wall.

'Who is this gentleman, Mr Barker?'

Richard laughed. 'We don't stand on ceremony in this household, John. Where I come from, people are straight with each other and say what they feel. Call me Richard, please. Pour us some refreshment and I'll tell you about him.'

John did so. Sitting in one of the two chairs in the room, Richard gestured for John to sit next to him.

'That there is Dr James Barry,' said Richard, indicating the portrait. 'A fascinating character who I worked with for about three years and who Olive met on numerous occasions too. You could say there was a connection between them. He was always so encouraging in his comments to Olive. She never forgot him. However, it is what we have discovered of him since he left Canada that has really inspired my eldest daughter, as well as adding poignancy to his legacy.'

John was intrigued, moving forward in his seat to better hear over the distant clang of pots and pans in the kitchen. Richard crossed one leg over the other and started his story.

'Dr Barry was a military surgeon, a damn fine one apparently, in the British Army. He was born in Ireland, but he moved to England and studied medicine at the University of Edinburgh. After qualifying he joined the army and served first in Cape Town, South Africa, where he performed the first successful caesarean section in Africa by a British surgeon. Then he went on to serve in other parts of the empire. Before he retired, he'd risen to the rank of inspector general in charge of military hospitals, the highest medical office in the British Army.

'By the time I met him he had established quite a reputation. Wherever he'd worked, improvements to sanitary conditions had been made for soldiers and civilians. He was outraged by unnecessary suffering and took a heavy-handed and often tactless approach in demanding improvements for the poor and underprivileged.

'On a number of occasions he was arrested, even demoted for his extreme demands. But his heart was in the right place. It was just the way he went about things that upset some people. He didn't suffer fools gladly; he just got on with his job. He kept you at a distance, and it took a while to get to know him, but I liked him and I was sad to see him go, not least because he got on so well with Olive.

'We said our farewells and he retired to London, where he died in 1865, ten years ago now. When you look back on his career, he achieved an awful lot, and no doubt he was justifiably proud of his work. Only "he" was not a "he". He was a "she".

John had just taken a sip of his homemade lemonade, and he nearly regurgitated it on the spot. Richard gave his guest a moment to digest what he had just told him, before he went to a shelf of periodicals and papers and pulled out a document.

'Olive wrote it up. Best if I read from it. I'll digress at times, but it's a good read. Turns out when Dr Barry died a charwoman found him. This cleaner, who also laid out the dead in the lodgings she looked after, undressed the body and found the person who she had thought was a man was in reality a woman. Not only this, but Barry had stretch marks; she'd had a child too!

'Barry had left instructions that "in the event of his death, strict precautions should be adopted to prevent any examination of his person". He had specified that the body be "buried in the bed sheets without further inspection". She wanted to take her secret to the grave. She had a physician in London, a Major McKinnon, but he refused to pay the charwoman for her services. So she went to the press, and that is when the full story came out.

' "He" was really Margaret Bulkley, born in Cork, Ireland in 1789. Margaret's uncle was a celebrated artist and professor of painting at London's Royal Academy, and it was he who was the real James Barry. He died in February 1806, and so in time she adopted his name.

'It seems Margaret was taken advantage of in her mid-teens, and she gave birth to a daughter, Juliana, who was passed off as her sister. While Margaret recovered from the birth, her mother dutifully looked after her granddaughter as though she was her own daughter.

'Margaret had always had a passion for medicine, and loved the idea of being in the army. But neither of these careers were remotely possible then or even now. So her mother and some of her late brother's liberal-minded friends hatched a plan to enable her to enter medical school.

'On the 30th November 1809, Margaret travelled up to the University of Edinburgh, and along the way she became "James Barry", nephew of the late James Barry RA. Such was her commitment to medicine, she never again presented herself as a woman.

'Barry was short in stature and had an unbroken voice and delicate features, which led many people to suspect that she was a young boy not past puberty. In fact, the university senate initially attempted to block Barry's application for the final examinations, due to her apparent youth. However, the Earl of Buchan, a friend of the late James Barry, persuaded the senate to relent, and Barry qualified as a doctor in 1812.

'She then enrolled at the United Hospitals of Guy's and St Thomas' in London, where she was taught by the celebrated surgeons Henry Clive and Astley Cooper. And on the second of July 1813, she successfully passed the entrance examination of the Royal College of Surgeons of England.

'Having succeeded against all the odds in the first part of her plan, she then embarked on phase two, earning a commission into the British Army, which because she went in at officer level, did not require a medical.

'After military training, Barry was posted to Cape Town in 1816. Through Lord Buchan she had a letter of introduction to the governor, Lord Charles Somerset. The governor's daughter was ill, but Barry treated her so well that she was appointed not only the governor's personal physician but also colonial medical inspector, an extraordinary jump from her previous rank of lieutenant.

'This was over a period of time, of course. Barry was in Cape Town for a decade. But eventually she had to leave after Lord Somerset was involved in a libellous court case accusing him of homosexual acts with her. The governor defended himself successfully without revealing the real nature of the affair or the gender of his physician. But the damage was done.'

Barry was promoted to surgeon to the forces on the 22nd November 1827, and was posted to Mauritius, but she went absent without leave in 1829 when Lord Somerset, now in England, fell ill. She would have been court-martialled had it not been for her exemplary service. Barry stayed with the governor until his death in 1831, before resuming her military service in Jamaica and St Helena, where, after a flaming row with a fellow army surgeon, she was finally court martialled for "conduct unbecoming of the character of an Officer and a Gentleman". But she was found not guilty and honourably acquitted.

'After a number of other postings, in 1854 Barry requested to serve in the Crimean War, a request which was denied, whereupon she took annual leave and went anyway.

'In Barry's normal obstreperous way, whilst she was there she had a huge row with Florence Nightingale.

She ended up challenged to a pistol duel by Captain

Josias Cloete of the 21st Light Dragoons. Cloete missed but Barry's bullet hit the captain's military cap, removing the peak and grazing the soldier's temple. He survived, luckily for him!

'From there Barry was posted to Canada, which is where I worked with her as an engineer in the hospitals she ran. I think she liked my straightforward Yorkshire common sense. I invited her to lunch, and she and Olive hit it off straight away. She was much more animated with children than with adults, and she came to lunch regularly. Olive will— Oh! Olive, hello, what an apposite interruption. I was just telling John about Dr Barry.'

'Don't get me started, father, lunch is ready. Would you care to come through, John? As Dad has monopolised you, I've put you next to mum and opposite Annie. Is that all right?'

'That would be delightful. Thank you, Olive.'

As John was shown through the ground floor to the dining room, he tried to take in his surroundings. He had never been in a house as grand as this before. He realised he was being inconsiderate; he ought to initiate some conversation with Olive before they got to the dining room.

'Your father was telling me about Dr Barry. An extraordinary tale. And an extraordinary woman, by the sounds of it. Tell me, Olive, how you feel about her.'

'I liked her when I was young because she took an interest in me, talked to me, wanted to know what I thought. Apart from my parents, there weren't that many adults who did that. She was adamant that in life you should do what drove you, follow your instincts.

That you should be able to choose your own career. Now that I know what I know, I think I can truly understand her passion.'

Olive, John and Richard entered the room, which was a hive of activity. The sisters were laying out food onto plates. They greeted him, carrying on with their tasks as Olive continued.

'I think everyone needs to be loved and needs to love someone. How cruel then that Dr Barry had to resort to subterfuge for fifty-six years to pursue the love of her life, medicine, as well as suppressing any other desires she had. This is perhaps what embittered her during her later years. Who could blame her? Her story is such a sad one.

'Things are slowly changing though. Our doctor is Emily Stowe, the first female doctor to practice in Canada. How ridiculous that they won't license her! And Jenny Trout, who is a fellow Scot like yourself, in March this year earned her Medicinae Doctorate from the Women's Medical College of Pennsylvania. She actually lives in Toronto, but she and Emily were treated so badly while studying medicine at the university there, she no doubt felt she had to travel to get her license to practise.

'This is a leading question, John, but what are your thoughts on women in medicine – or in anything else for that matter?'

'Careful, John!' said Richard.

Susannah ushered everyone to sit. 'That's an unfair question to ask of our guest, Olive,' she said to her eldest daughter, placing a hand on the back of that of their guest. 'Would you do us the honour of saying grace, please, John?'

John smiled. 'Perhaps I can respond truthfully to both questions with the same answer, and still be here for dessert.'

Olive appreciated that John had taken her question seriously, and not shied away from an issue she cared so much about. If he weren't so taken with her sister, she might have contemplated him for herself. She liked his sense of humour, and he had shown he was not daunted by a spirited woman. Olive's forthright approach and combative style had dissuaded a number of pursuants; she felt sometimes she was destined to remain a *feme sole*. And she didn't care a jot.

John told them about his early childhood in Scotland. He was not ashamed of the poverty of his young life, because he had been enriched by the quality of his mother's guidance and upbringing.

'I felt lucky. The primary influence on me was my mother. Hers was a simple quest for spirituality based on trust, love and boundless optimism. She always tried to see the positive in what we did as long as we did the best for ourselves.

'She was a woman of great humility and would consider every angle before ever making a decision. She exemplified diligence and care in her thinking, and no matter what the situation she always had a considered response based on what she thought was right and wrong.

'She would not rush into matters; she would rather defer an opinion until she had given the subject sufficient thought. And she had a belief in my brothers and I that was relentless. If I were lucky enough to have a daughter one day, I would want her to embody these same principles, but in her own way, of course. I would like her to achieve whatever she is capable of, and not be restricted or held back by social protocol.

'Dr Barry, Emily Stowe and Jenny Trout perhaps dreamt of a utopian meritocracy. For that dream, they have sacrificed so much. It is not in vain. For where they have led, more will follow, and I, by my very answer, have talked myself into a conclusion. To rephrase the question, "Should you stop someone from following a career based purely on gender?" The answer, unequivocally, is "No!" I don't see this as a liberalisation of society in the political sense; it is simply a question of what is right and wrong.'

Richard sighed a sigh of relief. 'You can come to lunch again!'

At this everyone laughed. The young preacher's words relieved them. They wouldn't be arguing all meal long.

'You have talked extensively about your mother,' Olive remarked. 'What of your father?'

'I believe he was essentially a good man, but he was weak. Both he and his own father were undone by the desire to drink. But without knowing it, they have had a huge influence on my life. I have resolved never to touch a drop and make the best of what I have. I am a keen follower of the Temperance Movement that's sweeping these parts.'

'And what of the future?' Annie's eyes sparkled expectantly.

'I am here to stay.' The sentiment was in reality a half-truth, because John secretly harboured a wish to go to Fiji or Japan. But his answer placated Annie, who at the back of her mind was worried that John might want to return home to Scotland.

'When I first arrived in Canada, I was obliged to start work in a wood mill and develop my carpentry skills. The family I stayed with were very supportive. They got me involved in the church and gave me board and lodging. I valued what I learned, but I do not possess the carpentry skills required to make a business of it. And I needed my independence, so I rented a small place on Yonge Street in Toronto. It is a cobbler's shop similar to the one my family ran, and I live above it. It will provide me with a meagre income and support me as a student. I would like to do a Theology degree and be ordained as a minister in the Methodist Church. That would give me great satisfaction. I know that I need to develop my preaching skills – as you've witnessed yourself – so I will continue to work on the Park Hill circuit too.'

His host cleared his throat. 'It was on that point I wanted to offer some help after lunch. Susannah and I are Yorkshire folk, and people say you can still hear our accents, but when we arrived we were barely comprehensible. It might benefit you to let me listen to you read. I will offer some pointers as to how you might make yourself more understandable.'

John was never one to turn away from an opportunity for self-improvement. 'I would really appreciate your time and advice,' he said.

After lunch and dessert, and lively conversation that gave John license to talk about things other than himself, Richard and John retired to the library.

As John started to read, Susannah sent Annie in with

more lemonade, at which point Richard suddenly remembered he'd put down his spectacles somewhere.

'Back in a minute, Annie. Just get John to read please.'

'You don't need your glasses to listen to someone, dad,' said the oblivious Annie, 'and what do I know about coaching a voice?'

'Haven't you always corrected me when I lapse into the vernacular?'

'Well, yes, but—'

'Well yes but nothing. Crack on, I'll be back in a jiffy.'

' "In a moment", Dad, not a "jiffy".'

'There you are, you're a natural. Carry on, John, you'll find her an excellent teacher.'

And Richard closed the door behind him.

In the resounding silence that followed, the realisation that they were both alone with each other hit home with John and Annie. There followed an awkward moment where neither knew how to proceed. Then both of them started to speak at the same time

'You first.'

'No, please, you.'

They both said 'Okay' together, and laughing, John held up his hand. 'Let's follow your dad's instruction,' he said. 'I'll read, you advise. I would dearly love to hear what you have to say. And may I take this opportunity to thank you for helping to prepare such a fulsome lunch… And also to say how wonderful you look today.'

Annie loved his voice as it was, especially when it was complimenting her, and at this she melted on the spot. John smiled and started to read. Annie sat trying to gather her composure. There she was, eighteen years old, the youngest sister, trying to tell herself she was not in love with the twenty-four year old man in front of her.

Her ecstatic happiness extended to both of them, and gradually their defences lowered and they started to enjoy the privacy Annie's parents had afforded them.

Annie became bolder in her suggestions, John feigned indignation, and neither wanted their time together to end. John suggested that, for her to have a better understanding of what he was dealing with, Annie should try and mimic his accent. She declined but John was insistent, and finally she attempted her best Glaswegian brogue.

Annie had an infectious giggle, which quickly kicked in when she realised how appalling she sounded. John soon caught it too, and they both dissolved into gentle laughter.

Richard walked in over an hour later. His plan had worked.

Chapter Four

Enrolling as a theology student at Victoria College in Cobourg, Ontario, was the realisation of John's long held desire to study. Having overlooked the University of Glasgow in order to travel and begin a new life, he had now found fulfilment, and a direction that he hoped would ultimately lead to ordination as a Methodist minister, hopefully followed by a missionary post out in Japan or Fiji. But the best laid plans can come to nothing when fate intervenes.

Over his first three years as a student, John was as conscientious as ever, becoming as fully involved in the life of the college as he could be. He was a ready supporter and speaker in a variety of temperance organisations; he was elected president of the Jackson Society, the theological students' body; and he contributed both prose and verse to local publications like the *Christian Guardian of Toronto*, *the Cobourg World*, *the Park Hill Gazette* and the student paper *Acta Victoriana*. He used his own name as well as the pseudonyms Robin Rustler, Auld Killie, Old Gustavus and Samson Sing.

John developed his preaching and excelled at

Sunday School, where his enthusiasm and emphasis on fun drew in the numbers. In 1879 young Maclean served as a student minister at Grafton, near Coburg. Everything he had learnt, gleaned and developed whilst in Canada was thrown into this venture, earning him a report in *the Cobourg World* on the 26th January 1880:

'Great credit is due to Mr Maclean for what he has done in Grafton, by raising funds for a new vestry and other improvements to the building. He well deserves to be retained.

'The church is now one of the most comfortable and beautiful for its size in the province. And he has revived and reorganised the Sabbath School until there are now over one hundred children in attendance.'

The account reported that the church was so packed that people were standing in the aisles.

Unbeknownst to John, he was being watched by another preacher, a certain Reverend John McDougall. He was the chairman of the Saskatchewan District of Morley and Rocky Mountains Methodist Church, who, as John recorded in his journal, 'delivered a most interesting address on the manners and life of the tribes in the North-West, and the benefits they were reaping from the introduction of the Gospel'.

A fateful meeting had occurred between the two men, for the 'aggressive' Reverend McDougall was actively recruiting reinforcements for his missionary staff in the far west, and word had reached him of a plucky young probationer, John Maclean.

McDougall liked what he saw in the young Scot, and a short while later he pursued him to Victoria College with a proposition that was again recorded by Maclean:

'It was a common day, like all the rest of the year, and yet it was exceptionable on account of the singular experience which fell to my lot. I was sitting, poring over my books when the man with the slouch hat entered my study. In a familiar tone, born of little contact with men and constant communion with nature, he asked me somewhat abruptly when I would be able to start westward!

'I had indeed thought of going west in a year or two but it was to find the east, for there was a fascination about a foreign land which was sufficient to woo me from all the associations of home. It was the promise of helping people to a better life that was the inducement that lured me.

'His clear blue eyes peered into mine with evident surprise that I should be astonished at his request. When I faltered for a moment, he drew his chair close to my desk and began to talk.

'My case was lost when I allowed him to draw me away from my books, for he was a rare talker... I could see the Prairies covered with buffaloes, the Rockies crowned with snow, and the tramp of ten thousand men fell upon my ear. Of men with uplifted hands, pleading for the voice of a leader, of women crying for rest from their sorrows, and of children waiting to be fashioned into strong men and women.

' "When shall I get your answer?" he said.

' "Give me a week,"' said I, and when I had spoken, he smiled, put on his slouch hat and was gone.

'The room was dark, dark, and I could not see for the sentence of death was passed. I was in the Garden of Gethsemane, alone, contemplating being a missionary to unknown people. What about my Latin and Greek and French and Hebrew! They would be of no use in the Land of the Buffalo and wild men.

'My old college room became a veritable "vallis lacrimarum", a Vale of Tears, for Annie could not comfort me.

'And what would she say? Would she go to the Rocky Mountains to live amongst these folk? Would she live and, if needs be, die far from home and far from her sisters and friends?

'I passed some of my companions without greeting them, such was my quandary, and I hurried off to Guelph.

'I rushed in unannounced and, because I could not do any better, blurted out,

' "I am going west! Off to the Rocky Mountains!" There were tears in her eyes but a smile on her face and I knew without a spoken word that I would not go west alone.

'When John McDougall stood again beside my desk in my dingy room, he did not ask a question but looked into my face and with a quiet smile remarked,

' "We shall leave in a month." '

McDougall had got his man, but it took more than a month for all the practicalities of the trip to be arranged. First and foremost, John had to be ordained. But there was a problem: he was only a third-year student on a four-year course.

McDougall argued his case: yes, there were many fourth-year students about to be ordained, but none had the charisma or engagement of the young Scot. Once again, his fervour prevailed, and John Maclean's ordination was brought forward a year.

On the 6th June, 1880 there was a conference meeting of the Methodist Church in Hamilton, Ontario, to confirm the ordination of all those present. John Maclean recalled that 'at the reception of the young ministers I was called on to give my religious experience and cite my call to the ministry. As I was going to begin a new mission among the Blackfoot, I suppose my experience was interesting.

'My Scotch brogue seemed somewhat rough and unique in a Methodist Conference but had improved immeasurably since my arrival in Canada. However, I was brief and that helped me in my nervousness.

'At the close of the service, my old friend Professor Chancellor Nelles threw his arms around my neck and said, "I am so proud of you, Maclean!" The next day the members of the conference presented me with a purse which enabled me to pay up college debts, buy a wedding ring and choose a suit of clothes.

'Annie, my bride elect, was presented with some useful gifts from the school where she taught. It was a day I will never forget.'

A few days after that, on the 10th of June, 1880, John stood resplendently suited in the hallway of the Barker's home. He was nervous and, for the moment, alone. He could hear Annie's sisters talking excitedly in the dining room, whilst upstairs Susannah fussed with Annie's wedding dress, giving Richard's attempts at advice short shrift.

Footsteps on the stairs broke the spell, and Susannah breezed up to the man who in a few minutes would be her son-in-law. She took his arm and pecked him on the cheek.

'Ready, John?'

He smiled and nodded, and they opened the door into the dining room. The table had been pushed to the side, and half-a-dozen close friends of the Barkers sat or stood informally.

There was no fanfare, no great ceremonial announcement, but when John turned around the sight of Annie on her father's arm veritably took his breath away. John tried to take everything in, for it all seemed to be happening in a blur. He was coping emotionally until he heard the minister make reference to his recent ordination: 'And do you, Reverend John Maclean, take Sarah Anne Barker...'

Instantly everything came into focus. In the space of four days he had gone from lay preacher to ordained minister and from bachelor to husband.

Their honeymoon would be a trip into the unknown; soon they would not be standing amidst the trappings and luxuries of a beautiful family home, but in the depths of the Canadian wilderness. John could not know what exactly he would be taking his young bride into, but for him their adventure was everything he had ever wanted out of life.

John had been told that once he had built his own log cabin on the reservation, he would need to order from the supply depot food sufficient for at least six months. The wedding meal was as far removed as could be from the conditions they would enjoy as missionaries.

For the couple's honeymoon, Richard and Susannah had organised a suite for three nights at Frank's Hotel on Market Square in downtown Toronto. During their visit there was going to be a group of travelling actors performing – appropriately enough – Shakespeare's *A Midsummer Night's Dream* in the ballroom.

John's own dream was ready to be enacted, and the newlyweds returned to the Barker's house after a glorious three nights to themselves. They had to pack just one suitcase each for their long journey. As John was informed by McDougall, all their other supplies would be picked up en route:

'You need not take much with you from home except your books, clothing and such articles of bedding that can be easily packed. Your supplies and provisions can be purchased at Benton along with wagons to transport everything. They will be charged against your first year's salary.'

After emotional farewells, the missionary party left Toronto for the Canadian North-West on the 17th June 1880. The group was led by John McDougall, who had been made chairman of the Saskatchewan District of the Methodist Missionary Society, replacing his father, who had died in a blizzard whilst hunting buffalo in January 1876.

Also accompanying John and Annie were McDougall's widowed mother and four of her relatives, who were going to settle in the west. There were also four mission teachers and their wives, who would teach at schools in the forts close to the indigenous settlements. Additionally there were two tourists, and joining them a bit later, the Reverend Alexander Sutherland, general secretary of the Missionary Society, whose job it was to inspect the existing stations and look for possible areas of expansion.

The main party travelled by rail to Collingwood, and by the lake steamer *Frances Smith* from Collingwood to Duluth. This was where Dr Sutherland joined the group, and together they boarded the Northern Pacific Railway and travelled through Dakota territory to Bismark. This was the easier part of the journey completed, for they now had to travel by river steamboat at least 700 miles up the Missouri River to Fort Benton, Montana territory.

At Bismark there wasn't a river boat ready for them, and this gave the group an opportunity to see an American frontier town, of which John Maclean recorded 'that about every fourth building on the leading street was a lager beer saloon or tavern where there were crowds of men not very prepossessing in appearance, engaged in drinking, swearing, playing billiards and at anything at all to waste time, money and health.'

On Sunday the travellers gave an impromptu Methodist service in the city hall, as their own church was unfinished. The Reverend John Maclean gave his first sermon as a newly ordained minister, as Dr Sutherland recorded, referencing research he had conducted prior to the trip: 'the Methodist pastor spoke well and is doing good work in Temperance Reform, some four or five hundred having joined the Red Ribbon Movement through his efforts'.

The river boat voyage was slow, taking over ten days to complete. The passengers were promised an early sight of buffalo, but it wasn't until the sixth day that they saw a herd feeding. They initially thought they had encountered just a handful of the animals, but the herd turned out to be enormous; the buffalo were heading south and blocked the river for a day and a half as they crossed.

There was great excitement amongst the crew and passengers, who wondered if the captain would permit shooting from the deck. Permission was granted, and several kills of buffalo running along the river bank were recorded. John Maclean observed that his boss, John McDougall, 'stood on the Captain's bridge, and shot the buffalo as they were swimming innocently across the river, allowing their carcasses to float away. It seemed a heartless deed that greatly disgusted me.'

That evening the boat was safely moored, and the river lapped gently against its hull. Annie lay in John's arms in their cabin bed fast asleep, but he was restless. He carefully climbed out of their bunk, put on a shirt and went to take some fresh air up on deck.

The moon was bright as John quietly pulled himself up onto the captain's deck, where he found McDougall sitting in a contemplative mood, taking in the stillness and calm of the night.

Both men greeted each other sombrely; each knew they needed to talk. The elder man 'with the slouch hat' had an assuredness that wasn't easily questioned, but he'd seen his protégé's look of disapproval as he'd shot the helpless buffalo swimming across the Missouri.

'I offer no apology, Brother Maclean, for my actions today, but I will tell you my story in the hope it will enlighten you and perhaps give you a feel for the task you and your wife have ahead of you.'

'That would be useful. I had been hoping to talk to you about your expectations, and now seems as good a time as any.'

John Maclean had read in *the Toronto Globe* that McDougall was a 'thrilling platform speaker', and he had witnessed it for himself the day he had been offered his post. As the older man fixed him with his clear blue eyes, the young pastor felt intimidated.

'My father, George, was the son of a Scot like yourself, John, except he was born here in Kingston, Upper Canada in 1821. He was a farmer and then a Methodist missionary who helped the indigenous people in the negotiations that led to Treaty Six, liaising between the government and the tribes of Western Canada, to whom he was always a friend.

'I went to various mission schools and learned to speak Ojibwa when I was young. I, too, studied at Victoria College, Cobourg, and I, too, had my studies curtailed. My father needed me in the missions. I first went up to Norway House, becoming fluent in Cree, until my father decided we needed to go further west, for North Saskatchewan.

'So I've seen the destruction that advancing white settlers have inflicted on the indigenous tribes of Upper Canada. Though I believe it is a natural progression, and God's will, we have a duty to help these proud people in the face of this expansion.

'I have worked as an interpreter, a teacher and now a missionary. I have seen the hardships of life out here. In 1870, my sisters, Georgiana, Flora and Anna, all died in the smallpox epidemic that swept over these parts, killing thousands. A year later my wife, Abigail, died of the same disease. I thought she had recovered but tragically not.

'At the same time, the American authorities were

trying to get to grips with the whiskey traders, but they simply pushed them out of their country and into ours. Lawlessness fostered violence in the camps, and intertribal warfare intensified as the buffalo herds diminished.

'My friend Maskepetoon, who was a Plains Cree chief that I'd converted to Methodism, was murdered by the Blackfoot, and his Cree warriors sought revenge. It was a very difficult time – the strain was continuous, with disease, death and danger constant.

'I don't mean to worry you, John, for things are much more stable now, and I see bright times ahead. But there are a number of key issues that will complicate matters.

'Despite this massive herd of buffalo holding us up, they are on the wane. The repeating rifle has made them too easy to hunt. Buffalo can't sustain the tribes as they used to. The sooner they realise this the better, for as long as the buffalo is here, the tribes are harder to settle, thinking the good times may return. This is why I did what I did.

'Their only chance is their conversion to Christianity and their eventual adoption of European cultural values. In the reserves we need to show the tribes how to farm the land, which has huge agricultural potential. Where you are going could be covered with farmsteads and villages.

'These people need time to come to terms with this policy of integration so they can play full parts in the society that will prevail. They need to leave their polygamous ways and find God. The reserves will give them time away from the white man to realise the buffalo has gone. It will take a generation at least, and it is your job to help them through this important phase of their evolution.

'The North-West Mounted Police are established at Fort Macleod, and they will help stability in the area too. That is where you will be based, but you need, in time, to live amongst the Blackfoot on the reserve, for that is where they will accept you and accept the word of God.'

What both men were unaware of was that more than a decade earlier, in the US, President Ulysses Grant had come to an agreement with General Robert E. Lee that allowed soldiers returning from the Civil War to exterminate buffalo, hastening the demise of native Americans and making it easier for white homesteaders to expand.

John McDougall's words placated John Maclean. He could see the logic behind the older man's argument, although he was keen to see for himself whether the Blackfoot agreed with his assertions.

What McDougall hadn't told him was that the Reverend Henry Manning and his wife, experienced missionaries in a number of missions, had spent the previous year at Fort Macleod only to return to Ontario citing 'the general prevalence of vice and the lack of the restraining influences of civilisation, not least the absence of Christian mothers, sisters and wives'. They had had enough, and John and Annie were effectively their replacements. But even without this knowledge, John knew he and his young bride had a difficult time ahead of them.

The following day, the crew prepared barbequed

buffalo for lunch in celebration of their now clear river passage. Fort Benton was reached on the 10th July, but the party decided to camp two miles from town so that they had some peace and quiet.

John Maclean found the town a 'revelation' but for all the wrong reasons. It was a thriving distribution point for a vast territory. The young pastor noted it had 'saloons, restaurants, gambling houses and places of still worse repute. The main street was literally covered with playing cards, swept from gambling saloons after the night's debauch, where a new pack was used in every game as a precaution against marking them and thus gaining an advantage.'

It took the travellers two days to get all the necessary supplies and equipment to prepare for the last and hardest leg of the journey, which was by horses and wagons into Canadian territory. In his journal, John wrote of the discomforts of travelling in those days: 'the inconvenience of a bulky horse or two, mosquitoes and bull-dog flies, lack of drinking water for man and beast, combined with the weariness of travelling over the alkaline plains with the inherent dangers of fording streams and rivers.'

When they had to cross the Belly River at what is now Lethbridge, the area's lone inhabitant, Nick Sherin, ferried the whole party across, but it took a strenuous seven hours. After this, the mission teachers set off for their destination, whilst the Maclean contingent continued westward to Fort Macleod.

On this leg of the journey, the group came across Sitting Bull and his Hunkpapa Sioux warriors, who were still on the run from US authorities after massacring

General George Armstrong Custer and the Seventh Cavalry four years earlier in the Battle of Little Big Horn.

John Maclean commented, 'The day I met Sitting Bull I found a very sore eyed old fellow, sitting on a tummock with new spectacles, eating ice cream, and a more un-warlike man I could not imagine.'

Further on, as they approached the fort, they encountered many encamped indigenous people. This was the time for receiving treaty payments, and there were about eight hundred Bloods in the vicinity, receiving daily rations. Their numbers had been gradually increasing during the summer as small parties came in from the plains, where they had been hunting buffalo. Most were in a pitifully destitute condition.

Norman Macleod, the government agent for Treaty Seven commented in his journal: 'They have nothing except their horses and they will sooner die than part with them. They have no clothing, their lodges [tipis] are worn to rags and they are consequently drenched by every passing shower. They cannot even procure a pinch of salt to season their small ration of flour and beef with. There is no game of any kind to be got in sufficient quantity to be of any assistance to them.'

Not only that, but a large part of the Blood tribe were still on American territory hunting the increasingly elusive buffalo.

To get to Fort Macleod the party had to cross Old Man River, of which John Maclean recorded, 'A man swam our horses across the river while the ferryman took charge of our wagons and goods. The first sight that met our gaze was strange indeed. About half a dozen aboriginals were hooting and yelling as they swam down the river, their clothes being placed in a box which floated down with the swift current.

'Squatted on the streets gazing at us and chattering as we passed along were a large number of Blackfoot with their faces painted, a piece of cloth round their loins, a blanket thrown over them and a tuft of feathers in their hair, or cap if they owned one.

'Many of them were stalwart men with fine open countenances, but at first the ardour of missionary life seems to cool a little while gazing upon them. Nevertheless, we are here and ready to begin our mission.'

As John McDougall, his mother, and Dr Sutherland unpacked the wagons, they were greeted by Mrs Smith, an English churchgoer and wife of a reputable trader. She led John and Annie to their parsonage, an underwhelming small log cabin plastered with mud. It was about the same size as the summer house at the end of the Barker's garden in Guelph. After helping the Maclean's settle in, the onward party was ready to leave. Dr Sutherland, having inspected the fort as to its suitability for the mission, reflected, 'Brother and Sister Maclean accompanied us to the landing place and watched us as we crossed the stream. Those who travel together over these uninhabited plains, sharing mutual toils and dangers, form strong friendships, and there was a feeling of deep sadness in my heart at this break in our party.

'I could not but think of the isolation, the discouragements, the trials in store for John and Annie, who would have to grapple singlehandedly with the darkness and ignorance and immorality of surrounding heathenism.

'I saw Brother Maclean cheerily and manfully bracing himself for this arduous work but when my eye rested upon the slight girlish figure by his side, so lately severed from friends and home, I saw the quivering of her lip as her brave heart was choking back the tears.

'I confess my own eyes dimmed and I said within myself, "Thank God the stuff of which missionary heroes are made is still to be found in the Church." '

Chapter Five

The enormity of the task was fast becoming apparent, as highlighted by Dr Sutherland's inspection report to the Methodist Church, the people paying John's salary.

'The zeal of the missionaries who first made their way to this point is worthy of all commendation; but the wisdom of occupying Fort Macleod as a permanent mission station is not so apparent.

'McDougall, as chairman of this region, has consented to the appointment of a resident missionary but he seems to have yielded to the persistent representations of others rather than to the dictates of his own judgement.

'From what has come under my own observation, I am convinced that it is unwise to establish mission headquarters at any of these police stations. The officers, with rare exceptions, are opposed to our work and the men are hindered from attending services. Whilst not infrequently the missionary is treated with a marked disrespect which seriously impairs his influence and retards his work.

'Besides this, the task of evangelizing the indigenous people in the vicinity of these posts is attempted at an immense disadvantage, from causes too numerous to mention here. I think it very desirable that the missionary at Macleod should transfer the centre of his operations to one of the reserves at an early day.'

John Maclean was not keen on settling amongst the Blackfoot until he had gained their trust by learning their language. And words were only the start of it, for he would then have to justify their faith by his deeds.

He quickly realised that the social problems they would have to deal with stemmed from the disappearance of the buffalo and the signing of Treaty Seven in 1877. There, the Blackfoot Confederacy (Blackfoot proper, Blood, Piegan and Sarcee) had ceded their land in return for payments.

John had not, prior to his arrival, realised the extent of the problem. The Blackfoot, of whom he had been assigned to the Bloods, had been a free, autonomous, nomadic people, dependent on the buffalo for their living. Now in 1880, with the buffalo nearly gone, they were in a state of subjugation under and dependence upon the federal government.

What John had seen from the very first day was a people who had lost their sense of purpose. They were completely and utterly demoralised. As far as John was aware, they had not been given any choice about their future, and none of his superiors or the federal government were prepared to say they might have got anything wrong.

One evening, as they talked about the future, Annie spoke softly to John, 'I know we have to look back in order to go forwards, John, but you are expending too much thought on the past. Our lot is not to rationalise about the causes of deprivation, but to deal with the consequences of it.

'Regardless of the whys and wherefores, these people need our help. They are weak and vulnerable. We've seen the whiskey traders' exploitation of them. They need people to guide them. They need understanding, compassion and empathy. That is how to gain their trust and respect, and only by doing this will we make them believe they have a future in these parts.' She banged the table with her fists. 'We have to give them hope, for without hope where would any of us be? Sermon over!'

Lovingly, John wrapped his wife in his arms. 'You speak such good sense, Annie. You have your father's balanced perspective and your mother's emotional intelligence. I am so glad you married me.'

John's job, he had been told, was to convert the First Nation people to Christianity, showing them the ways of the white man by teaching them to work the land and become farmers. In agreeing how they should approach this mission, John and Annie had devised their own agenda:

Understand the First Nation people (literally).

Show compassion for their situation.

Empathise with them.

Only then did they feel they would be in a position to satisfy what the Methodist Church wanted them to achieve.

*

One of the first visitors to Maclean's parsonage was Apokena, a tall, impressive medicine man 'who exercised the functions of his profession with success. Apokena is very friendly with white men and when he meets a missionary claims relationship because he too is a praying man. He is anxious to have his son taught English and learn the way of the white man.'

It was a mutually beneficial arrangement, where Apokena and his son taught the young reverend basic Algonkian words and phrases in return for the English equivalent.

Another boy, Akist, about ten years old, was employed by the Macleans to carry wood and water for them. He learned the English alphabet quickly and soon brought several other boys with him to be fed at the parsonage. Akist's real utility was in helping John begin to further grasp the rudiments of Algonkian, which at first hearing was 'a language that seemed a medley of confusion'.

Maclean's plan was to first make his mark from Fort Macleod, holding services in the church in town and starting a school in the same building. Establishing himself in this way would provide security for Annie, and from there he could venture into the Blood reserve and become better acquainted as his grasp of the language improved.

He noted a whole different type of linguistic skill as he walked down the main street in Fort Macleod, where 'intermingled with the scarlet tunics of the Mounted Police, the long hair and buckskin suits of the bullwhackers, the gay attire of the half-breed women, was the resounding Western slang of the frontiersmen – each of the men being an artist of swearing, vying with one another as a genius in words.'

The reverend befriended three mixed-race men who all worked as Blood interpreters for the North West Mounted Police, and they further helped him get to grips with the language.

There was Flying Chief, who had been adopted as a child by the trader Johnny Healey and had the use of his other name, Joe Healey. He became the first Blood to receive a formal education. Then Jerry Potts, also orphaned, the son of a Scottish trader and a Blood mother. And then there was David Mills, the son of a black labourer for the American Fur Company and a Blood mother. Missionaries were given a budget for language lessons, and Maclean spent every other evening with one of his translators, making notes of what they taught him.

Somewhat optimistically, Maclean sent Akist with one of his older friends to go around the lodges and invite people to a meeting in the church at Fort Macleod in a week's time, on a Sunday afternoon. A little to his surprise, he was delighted to get a church full of men, women and children led by the head chief, Red Crow, and four other chiefs.

Using Jerry Potts as his interpreter, John outlined his plans for teaching their young to read, telling them about God and about his wish to be their friend, all of which went down well with Red Crow, who shook his hand enthusiastically at the close, saying how much he liked what he had heard.

This was a good start. To have any level of success,

Maclean had to have the blessings of the respected elders. Still he pondered what 'success' might practically mean, but he was reassured by Annie's summation: 'All these people need right now is help. Help reflecting on what has happened to them so they can cope with the here and now. Only then can they begin to look forward with some sort of optimism. If we can achieve that, we will have been successful.'

In this way, the Macleans supported each other, picking each other up with words of encouragement and practical solutions to the problems they encountered. They were both keen on opening a school in Macleod, but before they did so, John wanted to look at the one John McDougall had set up in his mission to the Stonies, close to what is now Morley.

The mission was about 150 miles away, but wasn't far beyond the northernmost point of the Blackfoot reserve, which covered 575 square miles and was the largest reserve in Canada. The reverend was going to have to get used to covering a lot of ground on horseback, and now seemed as good a time as ever to start.

When he arrived, he found the teacher, Andrew Sibbald, giving his pupils their lessons in spelling and reading. John's attention was drawn to one boy in particular, a heavyset lad whose answers indicated a quick mind.

'Who is that boy with the broad face and the twinkle in his eye?'

'Well, you might ask, reverend. He goes by the name of Little Bear or Walking Buffalo, which in his language is Tatanga Mani. He's quite a handful, but he could be a leader if we can guide him properly.'

'I'd like to talk to him,' Maclean said. 'The lad fascinates me.'

The reverend saw something in this strong and athletic boy. He had a spark that inspired the young preacher.

The boy's teacher elaborated: 'He is strong, very strong and wild at times, but he has gentle eyes and a benevolent smile that makes you forgive him all his impassioned inadequacies.'

'And what of his home circumstances?'

'I will enlighten you at the end of school, for it is an interesting story, which was told to me by a Stoney interpreter.'

Once the pupils had gone, Sibbald explained, 'Both of Tatanga Mani's grandfathers were tribal chiefs: Chief Abraham of the Wesley band on his mother's side, and Chief Meat Hunter of the Bearspaw band on his father's. The latter changed his name to become the first chief Walking Buffalo.

'Change of name is common in their society, as you probably realise, Reverend, with names recording experiences. Normally a mother chooses a name until her son earns another by personal performance, and that name could be changed again and again.

'Meat Hunter was a great warrior and, as his name suggests, a highly skilled provider of game for his tribe, but in his older years he formed some strong views about the folly of fighting. Had he not already earned the respect of his tribe, they would have seen him as weak, but because his courage was beyond question, they listened to him.

'His radical idea of living in peace with both

themselves and white men could not be dismissed lightly. Maskepetoon of the Cree created a similar sensation among his people when he came to the same unconventional conclusion, maintaining that it took more courage to be a man of peace than to be a killer. This idea seemed unthinkable to people who for generations had sought glory in bloodshed and intertribal rivalry. But the wise old Walking Buffalo convinced some of his tribesmen, including his nephew Jacob Bearspaw, to whom he passed the chieftainship.

'The young Walking Buffalo was inspired by the boldness of his grandfather, just as he was impressed by the tenacity of his own father, Wolf Ear. As a hunter, nobody surpassed the square-faced, heavily built Wolf Ear. When he went for fresh meat, he never returned without supplies. He would follow a deer or an elk for days, with the patience of a wolf, before finally felling it with an arrow from his quiver. Wolf Ear also possessed an enquiring mind. He would sit on the hillside overlooking the Bow River and study the landscape, watching hawks dive for mice, observing the deer and gazing at the clouds as they dropped hints of approaching storms.

'When Wolf Ear married Leah Abraham, their tipi was filled with happiness. She was cheerful, clever, an expert in tanning buckskin and making moccasins, and they were both overjoyed when she became pregnant. Wolf Ear's tipi was on a hillside from which the Bow River could be seen flowing like a silver serpent toward the prairies, and it was there on March 20th, 1871, while snow was still on the ground, that Tatanga Mani was born.

'The little one was washed in warm water, wrapped in moss and placed in Leah's arms as Wolf Ear danced outside, shouting his joy before dropping a shoulder of venison into the pot for the feast which would follow. The healthy baby nursed, kicked and cried, but there was something wrong with the gentle Leah. Her pain continued day after day, even when the tribal medicine man attended to her. Her condition deteriorated until, after seven weeks, she died, leaving her underfed son without a mother.

'Wolf Ear's grief was overwhelming. To lose his wife and now almost certainly his son... But Tatanga Mani's grandmothers came to the rescue, determined that their half-starved grandchild should live. Another newborn, Lazarus Dixon, was two months old as well, and his mother agreed to feed both babies. His grandmothers called him Little Bear, though his father preferred Walking Buffalo, and from a difficult beginning, he went from strength to strength, thanks to the surrogate mother who fed him until he was weaned.

'When he was too heavy to be carried in a moss-lined bag on someone's back, Walking Buffalo romped on the ground around Grandmother Jane's tipi, or sat on her knee to hear stories about wild animals, friendly trees, the changing moods in rivers, and the Great Spirit who made and rules all. It is the first step in a child's education to learn about the Great Spirit's world, in preparation for a lifetime searching for him.'

John Maclean was transfixed by the story. There was a connection between him and Walking Buffalo, in that they had both lost their mothers at a young age. John also loved the pursuit of spirituality in the story. It had a romantic mysticism that mirrored his own search for the truth. He encouraged the teacher to continue.

'All my pupils have learnt many practical things before they ever get to me: chipping flint, making fire, stalking game, choosing wood for bows and arrows, selecting herbs, learning how to fight... They have a fierce tribal pride that has to be tempered, and this is difficult. To preserve their tribal identity, the children are imbued with traditions and these are perpetuated by stories from one generation to the next.

'Tales expand with their telling, and it becomes difficult to separate fact from fiction. But the stories stimulate young minds and prepare youthful bodies for the tests of living. I have spoken to the children individually, and there are common threads that run through their culture. Dreams and visions loom large in their lives, always inviting explanation. Given their belief in the rationality of nature, the Stonies believe even dreams are purposeful.

'They talk of the Great Spirit operating according to a plan, and therefore visions have to carry messages. I regularly talk of the visions of Meat Hunter and Maskepetoon, who talked of living in peace with white people. It resonates with the young ones, but it will take time for these concepts to be imbedded in their society. Education is the only way. We cannot tell them they have to change, they have to discover peaceful ways for themselves. And Tatanga Mani is the ideal character to effect such change.

'He has great physical strength, but he is imbued with a keen sense of right and wrong. He has the courage to defend his convictions and will stand up to anyone if he thinks they are misguided. He will also support those who are weaker than him if he feels they are being unjustly treated by the older boys. He is thought provoking but also thoughtful. But while he has a bright mind, he has to be continually and purposefully engaged, or he's off to learn more from the Great Spirit. I don't see him for a few days, and that's his way of telling me he's bored.

'He is a wanderer, you know. The first time occurred when he had just learned to walk. He had been playing close to Grandmother Jane's tipi, while Jane was busy with her chores. After a while, she noticed Little Bear was nowhere to be seen. She called his name, checked in and around the tipi, all to no avail. She went around the other lodges, and her friends joined in the search, combing the tree-covered ground close to the Bow River. Still no sign.

'Darkness descended upon the mountains and valleys, and the possibility of a tragedy crossed the mind of every Stoney. Could it be that a hungry wolf or she-bear had emerged from its forest home to carry the child away? Had he fallen into the churning river, or was he simply hiding and waiting to be discovered?

'The following day, Wolf Ear got the medicine man to help, and at first light the search was resumed. They looked all day, but as it got dark, still there was no trace of the child. So the medicine man counselled the group to appeal to the Great Spirit.

'A fire was built in a clearing, and they gathered around it in a circle. Scalps and eagle heads dangled from Wolf Ear's belt, and the medicine man's face was painted and partially masked by a headpiece made from crow's wings.

'Advancing towards the fire, the medicine man threw incense into the flames, and with the air of a man enjoying his own authority, demanded silence, then ordered singing and the smoking of pipes. Finally he called on the Great Spirit to tell him whether or not Walking Buffalo still lived and, if so, where he could be found.

'There followed a moment of stillness when all seemed calm, until a gust of wind picked up, driving though the woodland, rustling the leaves until it was transformed into a voice that said, "The boy is alive and will be found with the buffalo herd."

'There were many herds, and only occasionally did they venture up to the higher reaches of the Bow River. Generally, when Stonies hunted buffalo, they went east to the plains.

'Scanning the night sky, they saw a blue star in the east. This was their clue. They marked its easterly direction, and early next morning set out on horseback towards the plains.

'They saw buffalo to the north and south, but the medicine man stayed true to his eastern course. As the days passed, their travels took them into Blackfoot territory, where attack was always imminent. Finally a big herd was spotted directly east. They advanced stealthily so as not to make the animals stampede, and as they closed in, sure enough, the Stonies spotted a small boy playing with the buffalo calves.

'Wolf Ear impulsively called out to his son, and this startled the herd, who put their tails high in the air and fled except for one old cow, who stood close to where the small boy had been playing. Fearlessly, the cow faced them as Tatanga Mani ignored his father's calls and walked after the buffalo. The cow risked her own life by standing still, blocking the little boy's path, keeping him there until his father was close by.

'Speaking to them (as wild animals often did) she said she had found the waif alone in the foothills and had known he needed to be looked after and fed. She nursed him along with her bull calf, and when the herd moved, the child followed. Now she was returning him to human care. But Walking Buffalo didn't want to leave her. He had drunk rich buffalo milk, played with calves, slept with his body resting securely against the cow's warm flank and become a part of the animal community.

'Wolf Ear was distressed that his son still wanted to be with the buffalo, so the medicine man lit a fire, uttering the necessary incantations, and Walking Buffalo eventually relaxed into his father's arms, glad to be back amongst his own people.

'It's a wonderful story, John, and indicative of how these people approach life. The possible and the impossible commingle in the wonderful world around them, and they seldom try to separate them.'

The following day, the reverend observed Tatanga Mani in school again, and this time spoke to him at length. There was an instant rapport between them, and a thought entered John's head. He and Annie had talked about adopting a child. Some missionaries did this as a spiritual and not a physical commitment. In other words, the child stayed where he or she was but had another name to draw upon if it suited them. It was effectively a mentoring role, as opposed to a parental responsibility.

John talked about it with Tatanga Mani's teacher, who thought it an excellent idea.

'Walking Buffalo needs positive role models, people who can make him think about his role in society, not just his standing within the Stonies. We must take the idea of adoption to his father, Wolf Ear, and his grandmothers to see what they think. Not least, we have to talk to Tatanga Mani, for if he does not think it a good idea, it is not going to happen.'

John McDougall also approved of the idea, and went with Sibbald and Maclean to see Wolf Ear and the grandmothers to explain that the reverend would send Tatanga Mani clothes, see him every couple of months, and try to be a positive influence on the young boy's life. John would also give the boy a name if he so wished.

Tatanga Mani did wish, and so did everyone else. That evening Walking Buffalo also became George Maclean. It was as simple as that.

Chapter Six

The journey back to Fort Macleod took a few difficult days. John Maclean was struggling to come to terms with his new, primitive environment. The nearby Rocky Mountains provided a barrier, assuring the region of a continental climate with cold winters and short, cool summers. When the Chinook winds blew through, it could be balmy and warm, but when the winds came down from the Arctic, there could be dramatic shifts in temperature, making prairie travel hazardous, particularly in winter.

The dominant feature prior to white settlement had been grassland, with eighteen million acres of mixed prairie. Few trees grew, and buffalo, pronghorns and plains grizzlies were ever present. At up to 1,370 metres above sea level at its highest point, the surface was not simple to negotiate. The reverend had to try and cope with flat-topped hilly regions, rolling upland areas, as well as irregular lowlands interspersed with swamp-covered marshland. He recorded it thus:

'As I travelled, it was now a continuous climbing of bad hills, running over rough trails on the hillsides, sinking in bogs, tearing through heavy brush and scampering down the hills. I experienced the usual trials of wilderness camping: shooting at game birds and missing, fishing all afternoon in the Old Man River and returning wet and weary minus the fish. Making camp bread was my only solace, as it was pleasant indeed to partake of before I would set off on more treacherous creek crossings and steep hills.'

At nightfall his saddle was his pillow and the saddle blanket a covering for him. Before sleeping, he would make sure he put out the fire and survey the prairie for grizzly bears or wolves. His horse was an early warning system and would stir if anything approached whilst he was asleep; nevertheless, he would always lie down with his rifle by his side before he breathed a prayer for Annie and got as much sleep as he could.

On his return, John had been away nearly two weeks. He was overjoyed to see Annie, who knew she was going to have to get used to her husband's visits to the outer reaches of the Blood reserve. In his absence, she had busied herself making sure the church, which was to double as a school, was clean and prepared for the children it would soon be educating.

They had talked about having their own children but felt it better to try and wait until they were outside Fort Macleod and on the reserve. The Bloods had changed their minds about the siting of their reserve. Originally, in 1877 after the signing of Treaty Seven, when they believed the buffalo to be more plentiful, they had wished to be closer to the plains, where they could hunt. For each one of the previous twenty-five years, as many as one hundred and fifty thousand buffalo hides had been shipped down the Missouri to St Louis. But by 1884 there were just three hundred and fifty skins shipped.

Since time immemorial, the Blackfoot had hunted buffalo on foot, but around 1730 they had acquired the horse from Spanish explorers and quickly became masters at hunting on horseback. By 1800, 'The Tigers of the Plains' were successfully defending a vast area against invasion from other tribes and the white man. The Blackfoot had fearsome reputations as warriors, and free trading posts were kept to the periphery of Blackfoot control, anxious not to incur their wrath.

So the Blackfoot Confederacy controlled land that extended westwards to the foothills of the Rockies, north to the Saskatchewan River, east to the Red River and south to the Missouri River. Yet it was an area now barren of buffalo, so much so that two thousand Blackfoot had gone into American territory to chase one of the last big herds, the same one that had interrupted John Maclean as they travelled up the Missouri. At some point, they would have to come home, resigned to having to find an alternative way of life.

Against this backdrop, John and Annie opened the school in Fort Macleod, sharing their teaching in the belief it was the first small step in solving 'that most difficult of conundrums that requires the intellectual emancipation of these people and its natural sequel – their elevation to a status equal to that of their white brothers'.

After a week of teaching, John and Annie were greatly encouraged, as numbers grew day after day. But at the start of the next week, they were devastated when not one of their students turned up. The fort, too, was eerily quiet, and so they made enquiries as to where everyone was. They were informed that the Sun Dance was being held at the Piegan reserve, eight miles away. John got on his horse to go and see for himself this ceremony that he had heard so much about.

'There were over eighty lodges arranged in a beautiful valley with what seemed to be over one thousand head of horses and a large number of cattle. In the midst of the camp was a large lodge made of trees and covered with branches. In the centre of this stood a pole, near to which were two fires burning. At one side were six or eight young men tum tumming on drums. All around the lodge sat men and women on the ground, and in the innermost circle, close to the pole, were about a dozen chiefs.

'Right opposite the opening of the lodge was the bower of the medicine man. In this he danced and blew a small wooden whistle. I recognised my friend Apokena as the medicine man and was told he was not allowed to eat food during the whole time the camp lasted, which was a week. He only had water to drink and tobacco to use during that time but he was to receive four horses for his week's work.

'When I arrived a dance had started, after which was some wrestling. After each bout a young man would step to the front and tell the audience how many scalps of the enemy he had taken and how many horses he had stolen. Some of the men carried sticks with tufts of buffalo hair fastened to them, each tuft representing the scalp of the enemy which the bearer had taken.

'Men and women were dressed in their best clothing,

of which they have very little, but there was an abundance of paint and a profusion of feathers – I even saw an old man dressed up with a Scotch cap on, which amused me greatly.

'I went up the following day and saw young men wanting to be warriors. They had holes cut in their back through which sticks were placed. These were attached to ropes and swung in the air until the flesh gave way. Apokena, the medicine man, was still in his bower but there was a man on each side of it guarding him lest he should eat anything. He indulged occasionally in a smoke and seemed not much the worse for his long fast.'

At the start of the next week, the young men resumed their studies in school, much to the relief of John and Annie, who immersed themselves in their roles of tutors. Among their students were Sarcee, Piegan, Blackfoot and Bloods, several Métis boys and girls and one white boy. Few of them spoke English, so the few that did acted as interpreters.

The day would start with registration, but the Blackfoot students would not give out their own names. The reverend asked their companions to do so, but most of the children had two names, one honouring the child and the other mocking him or her. When asked, their companions invariably gave the name that made fun of them. This caused much laughter and nearly a number of fights, so John and Annie made a special effort to learn all the names that honoured each child.

The couple found that this engendered a sense of trust and mutual respect between pupil and teacher. They adopted a firm but fair approach, for they knew that if they didn't engage with their students, making the experience beneficial to them, they simply would not turn up.

John Maclean's Sundays were often hectic:

'I visited the club-room, restaurant, barber's shop, houses and lodges to seek out my congregation', but the people in Fort Macleod were generally indifferent to religion, and it was a hard task to entice people to his Sunday morning service. After this first service, Sunday School was held, and then another sparsely attended service in the evening.

On one Sunday, he rode twenty miles to the government mill for morning service with the employees, then a further ride of fifteen miles to the police farm for afternoon service, followed by a seven mile hack for an evening service at the reservation farm, where men were taught the rudiments of the agricultural skills they would need in the future. John would camp there and return home on Monday morning.

He had noted how few recreational opportunities there were for young off-duty policemen. The large majority were unmarried men in their twenties and thirties, so John 'thought of devising some method of giving them food for the mind, besides taking them away as much as possible from unholy associations'. He designed a programme of further education involving an address every other Wednesday evening in the church, and an evening school three nights a week in the police post.

He wrote, 'Knowing that there was little religious reading in the community, I took out my printograph and started a small double-sheet monthly publication, giving it the illustrious name of 'The Excelsior'. I am thus able to strike at local sins, gather North-West religious matters and, when I go to distribute them, I can put in a word that may get someone to attend church or lead them to Christ.'

It was the start of a career in studying and publishing that would last until the day he died. At the end of their first two month period, the reverend summarised as follows:

'Preached thirteen times. Lectured on three occasions. Lodges visited – two hundred. Miles travelled – about five hundred. Articles written for press – four. Taught school nearly every day. Edited 'Excelsior' and struck off fifty copies. Studied some college work. Studied the Blackfoot language. Gave away a number of tracts and papers. Letters written – thirty. Books read – four.'

Although John had been ordained a year earlier than expected, he had not graduated with his degree and so had to complete his studies whilst he worked. Exams would be taken periodically in Morley, which meant his having to travel back there on a regular basis. He was keen to return anyway, because he had ordered a buckskin suit from a Stoney craftsman, which he wanted to wear on his travels. Also, it would allow him to check up on his adopted son, Walking Buffalo.

But on his return to the Stoney reserve, he discovered that any hopes he had harboured of acting as a steadying influence upon Tatanga Mani had been grossly overestimated.

Andrew Sibbald, Walking Buffalo's trusted teacher, had left after his wife had tragically contracted typhoid fever and died quickly after. The distraught tutor had felt he needed a fresh start and departed once a replacement teacher had been found.

Mr Rowett was short, slim and austere. Single and in his fifties, he had done a variety of jobs within the church, moving on every few years. He had come into teaching later in life and was prepared to go where others would not.

He had an implicit belief in the power of corporal punishment, and unruly pupils were regularly whipped with a short strap of leather. Unable to hide his contempt for the man, Walking Buffalo was regularly singled out for beatings.

Since his adoption, in school Tatanga Mani had been known by everyone as George Maclean, but Mr Rowett felt giving him a white man's name was inappropriate and covert, something the young man could hide behind when it suited him. Instead of bringing the students into line, Mr Rowett's stance had the opposite effect, exacerbating some of the fractious rivalries that always surface at one point or another in schools.

One lunchtime, the pupils were playing soccer on the scrubland as Mr Rowett ate inside. George was a talented player, who had pace, acceleration and swerve when dribbling with the ball. He loved to play and gave full vent to his competitive nature. It was one of the things that made him turn up for school.

Whilst the group of friends played a good natured game, three older boys spectated, and very quickly their shouts from the side became derisory and insulting. The players initially agreed to ignore the persistent defamations, but when one goalkeeper let in a goal between his legs to the ridicule of the trio, George could stand it no longer. He approached the biggest of the miscreants to suggest he went in goal to see if he could do any better, before quickly withdrawing the offer, suggesting that the boy was too cowardly to put himself in the firing line.

The thug was much bigger and older than George, and set after the young Maclean boy to put him in his place. George side-stepped him easily, his lower centre of gravity making the pursuer look clumsy and foolish. Everyone laughed at the cumbersome boy unable to catch the upstart. It was an incendiary act that only infuriated the older boy further. He redoubled his efforts but failed to lay a hand on George, who skipped away from him like a rabbit being chased by a wolf.

But George knew he was going to have to face his adversary eventually. He slowed and turned, lifting his head as if to signal he was ready for hand-to-hand combat. The older boy was trying to catch his breath, his hands on his thighs, his large shoulders rising and falling. He didn't even notice George running at full tilt towards him.

George bounced off him, landing on his back. Seeing his opportunity, the older boy laughed, bringing his elbows up to try a body slam on the prostrate Maclean.

George rolled adroitly to avoid his antagonist's blow, and the older boy hit the ground, hard, winding himself.

George flipped to his feet, and as he stood over his groaning opponent, unleashed a barrage of quick-fire punches into the boy's face, splitting his eyebrow and drawing blood.

He worked the body, pummelling short jabs into the ribs as the older boy turned turtle to avoid further damage. But suddenly, rolling onto his front, his opponent kicked out to the side and George went down.

The two wrestled for supremacy, but in the end the superior weight of the older boy told. He heaved himself over Maclean, who was now close to exhaustion. George could do nothing as the older boy sat on his chest, pinning his shoulders to the floor, and took aim.

The only movement George could make was to twist his face from side-to-side, a fruitless exercise as bony knuckles thudded into the soft flesh of his broad cheeks. The older boy wallowed in his dominance, hollering triumphantly as punch after punch landed on George's rapidly deteriorating face.

'Give in and I'll stop!' said the older boy.

'Give in to you? Never!'

As he complacently enjoyed the damage he'd inflicted, the older boy shifted his bodyweight slightly, allowing George to reach into his trouser pocket. There he found the jackknife he used for all manner of things – cutting, trimming, skinning, but as of yet not killing.

With one last almighty effort, George swung his arm up to thrust the blade into the older boy's midriff.

The cacophony of squeals and shouts that accompanied this act created mayhem around the now semi-delirious Maclean. George couldn't quite work out what was going on, but he knew he felt more pain. Stinging, biting pain in the arm that held the knife.

He couldn't see out of his bloodied, puffy eyes, but this only heightened his other senses. He felt the weight of the older boy being lifted from his chest and then the same searing, slice of pain again and again.

Amidst the shouts and the sensation of being pulled

this way and that, George recognised the stinging feeling of Mr Rowett's leather strap, whipping him as so many times before.

George rolled into a ball as the teacher laid into him. He could hear his friends imploring Mr Rowett to stop. They reasoned that the teacher should attend to the older boy's stab wound rather than administer punishment to George. Eventually, save the slapping of the whip, silence befell the scene, everyone shocked by the level of violence exacted by all involved.

As, finally, he began to treat the older boy, Mr Rowett was almost contrite. His frenzied act of retribution had stunned everyone, not least himself. Luckily, George's knife had missed the major organs and arteries, but it had caused muscle damage. Mr Rowett managed to stem the bleeding until the doctor arrived from Morley later that afternoon, to further patch the boy up as well as inspecting George's soft tissue injuries. Both boys would recover physically from the incident, but the emotional damage would take longer to heal.

George was put in solitary confinement for weeks, and though he knew himself that he had done wrong, there he festered in his own pit of self-pity and vengefulness. Not for the older boy – their fight was over. It was Mr Rowett's extreme behaviour he could not forgive.

George's confinement was not the end of his punishment. He had to sweep the floor of the schoolroom, clean the school stove and chop the wood to fuel it. And one Friday after school had finished, along with his Stoney friend Sam, he had to accompany

Mr Rowett to the forest to cut more wood.

They had fixed a team of oxen that George led whilst Sam sat with Mr Rowett on the wagon. The oxen appeared more unwilling than usual, so George picked up a stick and tapped their hindquarters to encourage them to move faster. After two or three whacks, Mr Rowett jumped down and grabbed George by the throat, telling him not to harm the animals.

George was seething at the unjust hypocrisy of his teacher, but bided his time on the six mile trail to a forest by the river. At the end of the trail, George goaded Mr Rowett with a premeditated act. Apologising to the oxen under his breath, he struck one of them harder than before.

Mr Rowett jumped down and tried to grab George, who slipped his grasp and tripped him up. As he did so, George took a firm hold of the teacher's billy goat whiskers and held him on the ground. Meanwhile he threw the stick to Sam, who wielded it powerfully against the teacher's posterior in the same way he had done to them all. The boys swapped positions, and George prepared to exact his revenge. But as he moved to strike, George looked at the quivering frame in front of him, now begging for mercy.

George felt pity. The remorse he'd felt after the fight returned, and he knew that by using the same injudicious brutality employed by his teacher, he was effectively lowering himself to the same level. He had more self-respect than that, and so he calmly put down the stick.

George and Sam went about their work of cutting and loading wood in silence, the burden of the task falling directly to them because their teacher was suffering too much pain.

For the journey home the boys spread their coats on the load of wood to allow Mr Rowett to lie on his stomach and minimise his suffering. It was a small act of kindness that helped to reconcile the combatants. No-one spoke as they travelled back, all reflecting on the unseemly incident. Yet it was a cathartic moment for all of them.

At the end of the journey, Mr Rowett tried as best as he could to help the boys unload the wood. Still nothing was said as they laboured. The mood was conciliatory and reflective. Once they had finished, they stared at each other. Emotions were too raw to issue words of apology, yet their eyes were full of forgiveness and regret. It seemed they had reached an understanding of some sort, a point from where they could all move forward in a sort of grudging compromise.

Over the weekend, George thought about his actions, contemplating the repercussions that might arise from his folly. In an earlier generation, fighting had been the mark of a good warrior, but maybe the preachers Maclean and McDougall were right. Maybe George might end up killing someone, or maybe someone might kill him. Those churchmen said it took a braver man to be peaceful than to be a fighter. It seemed strange to George, but he was beginning to come round to the idea that they may be right.

The following Monday morning, Mr Rowett stood by his desk bereft of the leather strap which normally rested threateningly by his pieces of chalk. His chair had a cushion on it. George and Sam had sworn each other to secrecy about the incident, hoping against hope that the lessons learnt were mutual. They were right.

It was fair to say that George never liked Mr Rowett, and vice versa, but a more equitable working relationship had been established. The teacher never resorted to the whip again, and George was beginning to realise that compromise was, perhaps, better than confrontation.

Chapter Seven

In trying to understand the problems of his adopted son, John Maclean hoped to shed light on the difficulties faced collectively by the Bloods as a whole. By examining their behaviour from a more personal perspective, he wished to develop better strategies to alleviate their problems. His job and his extended family helped him to evaluate the Blood culture by his own criteria, and these ethnocentric studies truly fascinated him.

The reverend was now the proud owner of the Stoney-made apparel that he'd picked up in Morley, wearing it as he travelled on horseback around the reserve. In his own words, 'a strange looking personage was this sky-pilot dressed in his buckskin suit with his saddle bags full. In one of them his books and in the other, tea, sugar, bacon and biscuits. Fastened to the horn of the saddle... a small axe, frying-pan, rifle, lariat and picket pin.'

But to complete his outfit he needed some moccasins. As an expert boot closer, all he needed were the raw materials and some tuition. On one visit to Red

Crow's lodge he politely asked if some of the chief's wives might help him, a request that was met initially by disbelief and then by much hilarity. Moccasin making was traditionally women's work, and as a mark of friendship Red Crow instead offered John some of his own footwear, which Maclean declined respectfully through Jerry Potts, his interpreter, who travelled with him on some of his early forays around the Blood reserve.

Everyone found it amusing that a white man knew so much about the technicalities of shoe construction. But he was not the only outsider drawn to the sturdy footwear. As Jerry explained to him, 'The moccasin is the last thing these people give up... and the first thing adopted by the white man.' Maclean had seen for himself the mounted policemen in Fort Macleod all wearing moccasins, and when he asked them why, they had told him 'they were absolutely necessary in cold weather.'

As a shoemaker, the reverend noted the footwear 'allowed the Bloods full play to the elastic bend of the foot so that the muscles are well developed, leaving them soft, plump and chubby as a child's foot'.

The Bloods had two types of moccasin, which were designed according to their environment. The hard-soled moccasins were always made in rights and lefts, from two or more pieces of hide. The thick, hard sole was made from shaped rawhide and then the fitted leather upper, which required further tailoring, was added last. These moccasins protected feet from harsh cactus or prairie grass.

The soft-soled moccasins were often made from a single piece of leather, by bringing up the sole of the shoe around the foot and puckering the material around the instep. They were especially well suited to travel through woodlands.

Red Crow explained that, so distinctive were tribal designs and decorations, you could tell the tribe of the wearer by his footprints. Because of this, there were some tribes that added fringe trailing at the heel to try and obliterate their footprints.

The quilled and beaded decorations, which were highly valued, were designed so that they could be transferred when the sole wore out, whilst the flaps or added cuffs were wrapped around the ankle and held in place by leather thongs.

Red Crow's wives were beginning to realise this inquisitive individual, with his strange accent and gentle ways, was deadly serious about making his own moccasins. They were enchanted with the white man who took so much genuine interest in their craft. They showed the reverend some examples they were in the middle of making. John noted that the moccasins were assembled inside out so as to hide the stitching in the finished footwear.

'Women in making moccasins use animal sinew with buckskin. Whereas rawhide is used for the bottoms of hard-soled moccasins, the squaws brought the three-edged needle and sinew through the middle edge of the par-flesh, sewing very closely the stitches.'

Mindful that the spotlight didn't dishonour the chief by focusing entirely on his wives, the young missionary reverentially deferred to Red Crow to contextualise proceedings. Red Crow readily complied, explaining 'that when the Blackfoot went on war excursions in the south, far beyond the Missouri River where the cactus is plentiful and large, they wear hard-soled moccasins made of the raw hide of buffalo so the prickles are not strong enough to penetrate through.'

John then 'watched a woman shaving both sides of a cowhide to make a bag and moccasin sole. The shavings without the hair were carefully stored to be used in a soup, while I noted another girl who was expert in cutting very fine patterns of ornaments in paper to be used for bead ornaments on moccasins.'

With the agreement of his hosts, he took out his notebook and pencil to annotate his drawings. He saw that 'knots are kept on the outside for comfort and the whip stitch is commonly used in moccasin construction, often with a narrow welt running the length of the seam to make it stronger and help hide the stitching when turned inside out.

'Running stitch is also used partly, where the whip stitch is impractical, such as adding fringes. Seams are pounded gently flat in puckered areas.'

The more he watched and listened, the more he realised how important the moccasin was to the Bloods. Aside from practical considerations, moccasins functioned as a distinctive metaphor in their culture. Jerry Potts explained that, as part of a marriage exchange ritual, the Blood bride-to-be would present members of the groom's family with beaded moccasins worked by her own hand, after which she immediately took charge of the lodge.

War parties traditionally fought on foot, with each member of a party taking between eight and fifteen pairs of moccasins. As such they were an essential prerequisite for successful warriors.

Jerry Potts knew of one young warrior who sang to his lover:

'*Look at me*
My love,
I am just starting. Only cry a little,
I am almost gone.
Make me moccasins...'

'Making moccasins' was an expression signifying preparation for war, whilst 'sleeping without moccasins' signified a time of peace.

Jerry explained that the hide at the top of a tipi was particularly prized for making moccasins, as it was made more waterproof by the heavy smoke it was exposed to from the fires inside. The expression 'Now we have new moccasins' indicated that an enemy village had been taken, and the tipis or lodges could be cut up to make moccasins.

Red Crow was keen to add his own perspective. He cited the story of a Blood warrior who crept into a Sioux chief's tipi and ate food from the communal pot while the inhabitants slept. The emboldened warrior then ran off with the chief's horse whilst giving the war cry. To let the Sioux know who had performed such a brave act, the Blood left a moccasin.

John's visit to Red Crow's tipi had occupied much more time than he had envisaged, and he apologised for this. His humble politeness was appreciated by the chief, whilst the impact Maclean had had on Red Crow's wives was also plain to see. The women were used to hearing young warriors boast about the scalps they had taken or horses they had stolen, and they tittered incredulously when the reverend proclaimed with great pride about the moccasins they had inspired him to make. It was as though he were talking absolute nonsense.

Jerry Potts could see the humour in the situation, and congratulated John on the way he had communicated so effectively. As they rode back to Fort Macleod, Jerry tested John on Blackfoot words he had taught him, encouraging the reverend to use them whenever and wherever possible. It would show willing and help break down the distrust that existed between indigenous people and the white man.

The interpreter had taken a shine to the young preacher, not least because of his Scottish lilt, which reminded him of his late father's voice. John wanted to know more about Red Crow, and Jerry was only too glad to oblige.

'Appearances can be deceptive,' he began. 'Red Crow is now a man of peace, but in his earlier years, when he was establishing his reputation as a warrior, he was anything but that.

'His name is Mékaisto or Red Crow, but he has been known as Captured the Gun Inside, Lately Gone and Sitting White Buffalo. I could tell you stories about each and every one of these names, for they all tell of different chapters of the man's colourful life.

'He was born into a long line of Blood chiefs, son of Black Bear, or Kyiyo-siksinum, and Handsome Woman. One of his grandfathers was Two Suns, or Stoó-kya-tosi, who was leader of the Fish Eaters, the Mawyowi.

'In his early teens Red Crow went to war, establishing an impressive record, but he fell foul of the whiskey traders, who were pushing north out of Montana creating discord and bloodshed wherever they went. During one drinking bout he killed his brother Kit Fox and, in another, fatally stabbed two drunken men who attacked him. In the same altercation his principle wife, Water Bird, or Ohkipiksew, was killed by a stray bullet.

'In the aftermath, where some blamed the whiskey traders, Red Crow insisted they, as individuals, had to take responsibility for their actions and change their ways.

'So it was that he turned from a mercurial warrior who boasted, "I was never struck by an enemy in my life – not by bullet, arrow, axe, spear or knife," into a conservative leader. His leadership further evolved when a smallpox epidemic ravished the Blackfoot, killing his uncle Seen From Afar and his father within the space of a few weeks. His tribe chose him to succeed his predecessors, elevating him to chief.

'He became a broker for peace, welcoming the arrival of the North-West Mounted Police and forming a strong bond with their assistant commissioner, James Macleod – whom the fort is named after.

'Their friendship played a large part in Red Crow's acceptance of Treaty Seven, and he developed into a good politician, centralising the control of several bands of the Bloods and becoming their recognised head chief.

'So you see, John, Red Crow is a man of wisdom who has learnt from his mistakes. He is also a man of considerable influence. It is good that he likes you, but do not let his pleasant demeanour persuade you that he can be easily led. I have heard him talk to his people.

He is a warrior at heart, and he will not accept dependence upon the government for their future. He is the most forward thinking of all the chiefs and has told the Blackfoot they must become good at farming, ranching and educating their young people in order to become self-sufficient.'

'Wise words indeed,' remarked the reverend.

Once back at Fort Macleod, John was keen to show Annie the materials he would use to make his moccasins. Later that evening, as he started cutting the rawhide, he regaled his wife with stories about his youthful cobbling, stories that she'd heard may times before; nonetheless, she indulged him, because he was so enthusiastic and she loved him so much.

Playfully, her remarks became increasingly formulaic. 'Well I never... Did you really? How remarkable, John...' before the penny dropped, and her husband rushed at her and picked her up in his arms, laughingly apologising for boring her.

Annie was as light as a feather, but as he held his nymph of a wife so tightly, a look of seriousness furrowed John's brow. Annie picked up on it immediately and enquired as to its cause. John lowered himself into a chair, still cradling Annie, who sat on his lap enjoying their closeness.

'For me, this here, now, is the realisation of a dream. I have known hardship, and thoughts of missionary work sustained me through those dark times. I could not be happier to have achieved this position with you, the woman of my dreams. My worry is what I have asked of you.

'Your sacrifice compared to mine is immense. You

have given up your family and your home, nay, I should say, your entire way of life, to be here with me, and it pains me that I may have required too much of you.

'Think of the warmth of your house, the kinship of your sisters, the openness of your parents and the closeness of your companions. You wanted for nothing, and when you think about what was available in Guelph and Toronto, the less said about the food in Macleod the better.'

John could have gone on, but Annie, touched by his concern, placed her finger to his lips.

'If you are for comparisons, my dearest, let me give you a scene to dwell upon. Imagine that you had not asked me for my hand. Imagine that I, still in Guelph, was thinking of you in Macleod – can you imagine my unbearable unhappiness?

'It has been hard and, yes, it will get harder still, but be under no illusion that my place, where I want to be, is by your side forevermore.'

She kissed her husband passionately, keen to reassure him of her conviction, her loyalty and her love. It was what he needed.

The following morning, three young men came to their house to measure the length of Annie's hair, which she gladly acceded to. Young Bloods were especially proud of their hair and were envious of Annie's long locks. How were they achieved? What were her secrets?

They were captivated by her combs and brushes, and after asking her to let her hair down, they measured it using hand breadths. John watched the surreal scene, anxious to hide his mirth as Annie, clearly enjoying the experience, detangled, coiffured and rearranged the hair of the three braves.

The word was out, and from that day on Annie regularly entertained Blood men and women, giving instruction on hair care. On one occasion, several women came for advice while Annie was in the midst of a sewing project. John had bought some material from Morley, for Annie to make him a new pair of trousers, which, because he didn't have a sewing pattern, stretched his wife's ingenuity. There was far too much material left over to waste so, by pulling out a dress pattern, Annie was able to show John the preparation required to make clothes. He stood corrected and apologised.

Using chalk, pins and scissors, Annie was marking and cutting all the various pieces of cloth, at which point her visitors arrived. She gladly welcomed them in, and was about to clear away the material to create space for hairdressing, when a Blood woman pointed at the various cuts and looked quizzically at her.

Communication at this point was through sign language, the odd word and a willingness to understand and be understood.

Annie showed them pictures of how the finished dress should look and intimated how the segments of the jigsaw went together, which caused wonderment and delight bordering on disbelief. John watched with some amusement: 'it seemed strange to the Blood women that the garment should be cut into so many small pieces and then sewed together again'.

He later discovered that Blood women had a long history of making clothes from animal hides, with cutting and trimming kept to a minimum. As he travelled about the lodges, the reverend had noted that the majority of Blood women dressed in similar garments, but personalised their outfits, adorning themselves differently to create their own style.

'The Blackfoot women are fond of jewellery. Nearly all wear an old blanket thrown over them and from five to eight rings on each hand, or a piece of brass wire turned round the finger a dozen times to represent rings.

'While from the ears hang huge earrings and around the neck a very long strand of beads constitute nearly all the dress of a woman. Beneath the blanket they wear a plain gown of cotton without any tuck or opening in the back or front but with a wide overflowing sleeve, through which she can suckle her babies.

'The top and bottom of the garment is normally surrounded by a bit of red cloth as a piece of decoration, and a leather belt from ten to twelve inches wide studded with brass tacks encircles the waist.'

Both John and Annie kept their notebooks close to hand, so as to make English phonetic spellings of Algonkian words and build up their vocabulary. Nearly all missionaries created vocabularies and rudimentary grammars for their own use, but the reverend took this practice a step further. He had begun before he got to Fort Macleod, by studying James Evans' system of Cree syllabics. Evans had invented a system that represented sounds, enabling the Cree to read and write in their own language.

It inspired the Macleans to try and formulate a list of characters that represented syllables, which could be transcribed to serve as an alphabet. This could then be used to record words with their correct spellings, meaning and usage. It was an ambitious project but one they were committed to, for they believed a deep understanding of the language would give them a much better appreciation of Blackfoot culture, particularly their religious ideas and mythology.

In their shared effort there was much discussion to be had about the pronunciation and intonation of the Blackfoot language. One of their favourite words was '*tsûgkomitûpi*', which typically referred to something in the ground.

However, when this word was used in prayer, such as '*tsûgkomitûpikimokit*' it became an address to a spirit or deity, meaning 'spirit in the ground take pity on me'.

In this way, language was creative, open to interpretation; it was difficult to study, but its imprecision and fluidity appealed to the Macleans. At its core, the Blackfoot language was inextricably linked to spirituality, something the Macleans latched onto straight away.

Key to this was the concept that in Algonkian many inanimate objects, especially implements, were treated as animate objects. The thought that both humans and objects had souls was something the Macleans had never considered but found hugely attractive.

'As men on earth, when they are living, must live on material things – so spirits who are not flesh and blood, must live on spiritual food. The spirits take the spirit of bows and arrows and shoot with them, they eat the spirit of the buffalo meat and they smoke the spirit of tobacco.'

Smoking was important socially to the Bloods, 'who stopped work or travel to smoke whereas the white man smokes while he toils. The men always pass the pipe to one another in the same direction, and each man takes at least half-a-dozen hearty puffs, then one long inhalation and sends a long stream of smoke through the nostrils as he passes the pipestem to his neighbour. Whether alone or, more normally, in a group, men smoke long-stemmed pipes.

'Women also smoke in the same way as men but with a short-stemmed pipe resembling the travelling pipe of men.

'Decorated pipe stems are considered sacred and are treated under ritually prescribed conditions. The Bloods also have a tribal pipe that is of a still higher order. It has a large stone head with figures of animals carved before and behind and it is looked after by a woman who, when travelling, carries it on a horse upon which nothing else is allowed to be borne.

'If a Blood senses nearby ghosts who wish to smoke, he or she leaves a pipe filled with tobacco outside their lodge.'

When offered a pipe, the Macleans declined to smoke, but in all other aspects of their life they became fully immersed in Blackfoot culture. They believed that language was the key to their success. Their aim was not only to be able to converse confidently but also to speak Algonkian beautifully, believing the Bloods would then open their hearts to the message of the gospel.

They surmised that for Christian hymns to make an impression on the Bloods, both words and music would need to be reconstituted in a form similar to Blackfoot prayers, using fewer words and emphasising repetition.

The mission was in its infancy, but the Macleans felt they had established themselves. Annie had made their modest cabin feel like a home; John had a place to preach from that doubled as a school for them both to teach in; they had adopted a son, and they had an appreciation of what they wanted to achieve and how they were going to go about achieving it.

They liked the Bloods and felt a great affinity for them in terms of their culture and their way of life. Everywhere they looked there were challenges, but ones they were keen to embrace.

Although John knew that notionally he was the missionary, he was acutely aware that his success depended entirely on Annie. She was as integral a part of the mission as he was, and he wallowed in her resourceful, charming industry.

Chapter Eight

John worked as hard on his moccasins as he had ever worked on any pair of shoes. He knew Red Crow's wives would run the rule over them, inspecting every stitch, every knot and every detail. When he was as sure as sure could be that they were finished, and Annie had passed them fit for purpose, he travelled back to the reserve.

He was nervous, for he knew he would be judged – fairly or unfairly, and probably the latter – on his workmanship. He knew he would not be able to compete with the mastery of the Blood women, which had been developed over many generations, yet he was excited at the prospect of seeing what they thought.

The reverend knew he was setting himself up for a fall, but in his usual self-effacing, good humoured sort of way, he was up for it and in a playfully combative mood.

As he walked into Red Crow's lodge there was a genial air of expectancy. The women looked at John and pointed at his feet with raised eyebrows, muttering in Algonkian, 'Have you made these? Are they the ones?

Let us see!' Or, at least, that is what John thought they were saying.

John lifted his buckskin trousers to show off what he had made. His comical stance made him look slightly ridiculous, but he didn't care. There were murmurings of acceptance and incredulity. 'No! No! I don't believe it! Where did you buy those?' Comments he could only guess at, yet instinctively knew to be praise. The women approached, almost manhandling him to get the medium-sized moccasins from his feet.

The moccasins' size was the only average thing about them. They were immaculate, and John proudly allowed a closer inspection, revelling in the reception he was receiving. The women simply wouldn't accept John had made them. That was endorsement enough, and he laughed in his relaxed, laid back way. As the women turned the moccasins inside out to admiringly assess the cut and thread of construction, John was in a state of euphoria.

Red Crow watched it all in his unflappable, statesmanlike way, saying nothing but enjoying the scene as it played out before him. Then he settled everyone down, and said he had decided upon names for their friends. It was further evidence of acceptance. Maclean was to be called Niokskatos, or Three Suns. Annie would be Apawakas, or White Antelope

The chief elaborated on his choice. The physical sun represented the light of John's knowledge; the heart of the sun referred to his wisdom, whilst the centre of the sun, it's spirit, was linked to his intuition. Annie was dainty and nimble, with beautiful fair skin and tremendous strength of character, just like the creature she was named after. Their names bestowed respect and honour on people they were beginning to trust and admire.

The chief then spoke to one of his wives, asking her to fetch a leather bag. The chief rummaged around in it before pulling out some elaborate beadwork. The circular designs were said to represent a man waving buffalo into a buffalo pound. John loved the bright colours of yellow and light blue; his moccasins were plain and conservative in comparison.

He felt hugely honoured to be offered the beadwork by these people, who he now regarded as friends, and he made his acceptance clear. Red Crow signalled to two of his wives, who set about immediately sewing them onto the bridge of each moccasin.

The small congregation shared prayers in a meditative state. Red Crow rocked gently as he sat and chanted rhythmic incantations that the reverend, though he could not understand them, found reassuringly uplifting.

It was the same feeling he got from singing a good hymn with people who cared less for the technicalities of singing than for the spirit of the words. The reverend responded by singing to them in a low and measured manner. Shared worship, regardless of comprehension, was a spiritual experience enjoyed by them all – for the time being at least.

John heard horses arriving outside the lodge and the sound of voices, disturbing the peace of their prayers. He recognised the voice of Joe Healy, one of his interpreters, and another, western voice he hadn't heard before.

In a moment, the entrance to the tipi was pulled back, and in stepped Joe, with Samuel Trivett, a Roman Catholic missionary. With a raised palm, Red Crow intimated to the entrants to stand their ground. He wanted to conclude proceedings before conversing with his new guests.

The Bloods did not stand on ceremony except when it came to spirituality. Red Crow's wives had finished sewing the beadwork onto John's footwear, and the chief presented the moccasins back to the reverend with a gracious nod and a tangible sense of honour.

Samuel Trivett watched patiently as all this unfolded but was keen to announce his arrival in the presence of his competitor, the Methodist minister. John was anxious not to steal the limelight from another churchman and went to leave, but the newcomer stepped in to vigorously shake John's hand and thereby block his exit. At the same time, he bowed his head and removed the chain and cross from around his neck. Through Joe Healy, he offered this as a gift to Red Crow, who graciously accepted it.

Samuel Trivett then asked for permission to build a log cabin amongst Red Crow's band. The chief looked towards the reverend, who explained he was settled at Macleod with Annie and it would be some time before they felt ready for life on the reserve.

The chief nodded to both representatives, who were beginning to bristle in each other's presence. He reasoned that rivalry between the two would only improve the lot of his people – his primary concern.

Having entered the lodge in a buoyant mood, Maclean left deflated and demoralised at this sudden turn of events. Prior to his departure, he had offered Trivett the use of the church at the fort to preach in, a conciliatory gesture which had been politely turned down.

In a very short space of time, John's rival had made a definitive statement of intent: Father Samuel Trivett was here, and here to do business. But as John rode home, he wondered what that business was. Was it the business of vindicating a chosen religion, or was it to help these people? No matter what the denomination, the Christian ethic was surely to be selfless – to be there to help those that needed it. And the Bloods were desperately seeking guidance, divine or otherwise.

But John was pragmatic enough to realise that, in business parlance, those who paid his salary wanted to see a return on their investment. The thought was a depressing one, but for all the goodwill they had engendered, and for all the friendships they had begun, the Macleans would be held to account by people who could never truly understand the context or value of such work.

A short while later there was better news, when Chief Medicine Calf returned from hunting buffalo in Montana. He had heard good things about the reverend and asked Maclean to attend to his people on the reserve.

Red Crow occupied the upper camp whilst Button Chief, as Chief Medicine Calf was also known, occupied the lower camp. He had finally come to the realisation that the buffalo were on the wane and had decided to bring his followers home. Like other Blackfoot tribes, the Bloods were divided into smaller bands, and these bands frequently changed location depending on where the buffalo were. Now they were settling on the reserve, the bands stayed intact, dotted along a thirty-mile stretch of the Belly River.

The Reverend John Maclean wanted to stay friends with Red Crow and would visit him regularly, but now that the Catholic missionary Samuel Trivett had built his house in such close proximity to the venerable chief, the Scot decided to concentrate his energies in the lower camp, close to Button Chief.

The politics of the missionary game, which Maclean loathed, meant the twenty-something Blood bands had different allegiances, split between Methodist and Catholic camps. The reverend counted among those loyal to him:

Black Elks, led by Blackfoot Old Woman, Eagle Head and Stolen Person.

All Tall People, led by Eagle Shoe and Going to the Bear.

Scabby Bulls, led by Bull Shield.

Bad People, or Enemies, led by Eagle Rib.

People with Sore Feet, led by Strange Wolf.

Many Tumours (known by Maclean as the Sore Rectum People), led by Medicine Calf (Button Chief).

Much of his pastoral work involved travelling amongst the different bands and getting to know them. During one visit to the Scabby Bulls, Siochki, the young son of Chief Bull Shield tragically died after a short illness. It was the reverend's first experience of infant mortality, which he found a harrowing experience. He prayed with the family, first saying prayers in English, 'And then with what little of the language I had learned, [uttering] my first prayer in Blackfoot. It was a poignant moment.'

When they started to make their way to the grave, the father, Chief Bull Shield, stopped proceedings and said he wanted a coffin for his son, and for the reverend to say prayers over the grave once the little boy was buried.

John and a few helpers used an old wagon and some saws, hammers and nails to form a makeshift coffin. It took about an hour, during which time the women mourned inconsolably. As John wrote:

'I felt like shedding tears as I stood beside this strong man weeping for his son. Seven women and two men wailed in a most heart-rending manner.

'Then I prayed from the depths of my soul, "Oh God, help me with the language, that I may give hope and consolation to such as these". As I trembled and the tears filled my eyes, I cried in my soul. Light, light, send more light…'

Bread was placed in the coffin, some animal skins, Siochki's toys, a piece of buffalo meat and some newspapers before the lid was sealed and the body of the eight-year-old lowered into the ground.

It was a scene of unforgiving sadness for John's first Christian burial. He repeated his Blackfoot prayer, this time more confidently, and then said prayers in his own tongue before singing 'Jesus, Lover of My Soul', with all the memories that invoked.

John made a headboard from the unused wood and inscribed 'Siochki' with a knife. He comforted the family with the Christian belief in a life hereafter, which concurred with their own beliefs.

As he rode back to Macleod, the young pastor was in contemplative mood. Though saddened by the loss of a young life, he was nevertheless proud of providing some comfort through his inaugural burial. But his prospects in the longer term worried him greatly.

'This is not even the day of small things, it is the hour of darkness. These people have not been favourable to missionary operations lately. They have been asserting that ever since the missionaries began work, their children have been dying and they do not want the missionaries to stay any longer amongst them.'

His first burial would not be his last, and during this period Maclean would deal with death on a depressingly regular basis. Yet he was determined to show resolve.

'Despite the vast disparity of culture and belief separating Annie and I from these people I am confident of the Christian message we have to offer – we have energy in our bodies and joy in our hearts.'

As always the couple talked things through, Annie bolstering her husband despite battling with ill health through a bitterly cold winter. She was his sounding board, the echo of his conscience, and John's emotional lynchpin as he established their mission.

Life for Annie was bleak at Fort Macleod. But she knew theirs was a life in transition, and they were playing a waiting game. Her husband had started chopping and hauling logs from the Porcupine Hills to construct a school at Medicine Calf's camp, another at Blackfoot Old Woman's camp, with their house to be built in the former, close to the Belly River. Until these were built, she felt confined to the fort, where she had few people to talk to and felt conspicuous as one of the only white women in the town.

Although she enjoyed teaching in the school in Macleod, Annie desperately wanted to start a family of her own. They couple had agreed to try and delay this until their home on the reserve was finished. It was a holding game, and John picked up on his wife's frustration. Their situation was further complicated by Annie's ill health; she had developed a recurring chest infection that she seemed unable to shift, giving her husband cause for concern.

John was all too well aware of the dangers of a persistent cough, and he worried that Annie's immune system was not well suited to the Canadian prairie. His mother was never far from his thoughts.

Despite everything that was going on, they kept to a strict regime, with Annie taking rests as and when she needed:

'6.00 – Rise
6.30-7.30 – Devotion - Greek Testament and Breakfast.
7.30-8.00 – Theology
8.00-9.00 – Blackfoot Language Studies
9.00-6.00 – Manual Labour and Mission Work
6.30-7.00 – Writing Journals and Recording Notes of any Readings
7.00-9.00 – Writing Methodist Annual
9.00-11.00 – Letters and Literary Articles
Midnight – One chapter of Greek Testament'

Maclean also wrote to Dr Sutherland at the

Missionary Society to ask for financial help in respect of the building work he was undertaking; he would also need to pay teachers to work in his schools once they were built. This would remain a bone of contention between the reverend and the society for the length of his employment.

John had become acutely aware of the four key issues that he felt needed to be addressed if the region were to make progress. At first he published these rationales under various pseudonyms to avoid creating problems for himself. But it would only be a couple of years before he would throw caution to the wind and decide to publish and be damned.

The first problem was the casual 'common-law' relationships entered into by many white men and indigenous women. It was a practice of very long standing in the west, but Maclean, as he put it, was for 'proper marriage'.

'There are white men... who will buy women for a few dollars or a horse and live with them perhaps for years, yet when they feel disposed, will leave them for other women or go into civilisation, casting their children upon the charities of the camp.

'Why should not the law be enforced to compel these men to marry the women or in some way provide for the children and not compel the government to feed a large number of illegitimate half-breeds when the men are competent to support them themselves?'

The reverend gave an example:

'A white man, Major Brown, once of the English army, spent some time on the Blood reserve. This fine specimen of that educated class of his countrymen who, being possessed of private means, was able to indulge his desire for travel and adventure.

'He married an aboriginal woman and had a child with her. After some time the man returned to England "to attend to some important business". The woman with her young son goes back to her father who, after waiting two years in vain for Brown's return, sells her to an old man.

'The woman is not worth much because she has been the wife of a white man. As the fourth wife of an old man she enjoys the treatment of a slave, becomes ill and dies.

'Meanwhile in a large and busy manufacturing town in the West of England, a merchant sits in his office reading his letters. Amongst them is a paper from the Canadian North-West in which a parked paragraph caught his eye: "There died last Friday on the Blood reserve – Napiake, an indigenous squaw".

'Was she forgotten? No! He could never forget her. But in that busy English town where he is a merchant prince, married again and holding an honoured position in society... Little Charlie Brown, his son from Napiake, has to find a home, depending on others for food and clothing, and sometimes an old-timer takes compassion on him. He has to endure the poverty of a poor life, while over the sea, his father enjoys the comfort of an English mansion.'

Maclean suggested 'a goodly number of Canada's fair daughters would remedy this growing evil and be the salvation of the territory. For if nothing is done to destroy this squaw-slavery amongst white men the Government had better build asylums for the children and homes for the castaway women.'

The second area of concern for the reverend was related to the first:

'By the present system of feeding the aborigines, the Government has instituted and upheld polygamy amongst them and an institution of vice is established.

'Each person, from the babe to the veteran of three score and ten, is allowed one pound of meat and one pound of flour per day. The idea has been grasped by the men that the more wives and children they have, the richer they will be.

'Young girls of twelve years of age are bought by old men and live with them as one of their wives. Thus it is impossible for young males to meet a maiden in camp, for in the same tent are sitting side by side the young wife of twelve and the aged woman who has lived there as wife for forty and sometimes fifty years.'

Maclean wanted the government to be more proactive:

'If food was given according to the condition of work and amount done, it would not be so expensive to the Government and it would be very beneficial to these people. Furthermore the powers that be should encourage industry on the reserves by promising to buy the produce raised by individuals.'

John's third worry was that the North-West Mounted Police required greater support to protect the interest of both the white man and the aborigine.

'Fleecing of the aborigine should be stopped. In some parts of the territory the contract for flour with merchants is very high and yet the flour is of an inferior kind. It is very dark and almost unfit for use.

'Who is the gainer by this trick of trade? Does the Government pay a high price for a poor quality or is there some middleman enjoying the profits? The cattle supply for them is also worthy of being looked into. It is unfair if the poorest and worst of stock should be handed over to them for food. Detectives are needed for the reserves.

'I am for absolute fairness, for is the North-West Mounted Police only in the country for the protection of the indigenous people? No! More diligent and efficient policing is required for the white population too. Settlers close to the reserve have complained that numbers of their cattle, about two hundred or three hundred head, have been killed.

'It must be remembered that these people have led a roving life, that they have been accustomed from infancy to regard other men's cattle and horses as fair plunder and that the habits of a lifetime are not easy to unlearn.

'It is not natural to suppose that they will at once settle down to a quiet hum-drum life and devote themselves heart and soul to farming.

'Discontent may, in fact more than probably will, break out and the spirit of unrest show itself, particularly among the young men, which, if not suppressed in time, will result in periodical raids on the cattle and horses of settlers.

'This is why the police need support. Equally, my heart is made sad at seeing the amount of drunkenness that prevails here.'

This was the fourth key issue for Maclean:

'Yesterday and today I witnessed seven or eight cases

of drunkenness and this is a country where liquor is prohibited. Heard of one man who owed ninety dollars for liquor – I have an idea where it is obtained but have not yet seen it sold. According to reports in town the Mounted Police are as bad as civilians in taking liquor.'

Liquor permits could be granted on application to the Lieutenant-Governor for medicinal uses, but the system was rife with abuse. As the reverend commented:

'Let us not speak of prohibition when hundreds of permits are granted by the Governor of the Province, when not one per cent of the liquor is used for medicinal purposes. The aborigine is never granted a permit and if entire prohibition is seen as necessary to these people's prosperity so too can the white's labour and live and rejoice in the benefits of total abstinence.

'If we cannot get prohibition, take away this ludicrous system which is the North-West curse or devise some better means for ridding us of this evil and bestowing upon us the liberty we want.'

These social problems, which were published in 1882 in Maclean's first book, *Lone Land Lights*, were set against what Maclean saw as John McDougall's priorities: conversion of the aboriginals to Christianity and their adoption of European cultural values.

The reverend was not so sure:

'We wish to make them white men and they desire to become better aborigines. They believe that native culture is best suited for themselves and at the moment care not to give it up for an untried system. There is a real danger of educating them away from their real life.

'When you look how long it has taken to evolve the white men of today from Picts, Scots, Goths and Huns of the fifth and sixth centuries, it is only ignorance that could expect the same of them in one or two decades.

'God's spirit alone can touch the heart effectually, but we are striving to do our part toward Christianising and civilising them. I am trying by God's help to make intelligent and upright people, not trying to make them refined white men.'

Chapter Nine

In publishing his book *Lone Land Lights*, Maclean was hoping to raise funding for the schools he was building. As he explained to the Missionary Society:

'I am building mission premises near the Belly River, but I am also erecting a school in Blackfoot Old Woman's camp. There are about four hundred people in this camp. Could you not give us a lady teacher at once and a male teacher for the school in Button Chief's camp? We need a bell for each school and one thousand dollars for our buildings.

'Should the necessary help be sent me I can then devote my time to the spiritual interests of the Bloods and to the fencing and improving of the mission property together with the erection of all the necessary buildings.

'The amount of money is large but I assure you that three times that sum will not cover the expenses of the necessary buildings and appurtenances of the mission.'

Maclean concluded his letter here, but he continued this train of thought in his journal:

'I have been very busy getting out logs for the school. After taking my waggon in my boat across the river and swimming my horses, I had to go three miles and toil hard at very heavy work. For several nights I could hardly move. My arms and body were so tired and sore it was almost next to impossible to sleep but I got through a great part of the work with the help of an aborigine.

'However, received notice by last mail that I had graduated with a First Class Bachelor of Arts Degree in Theology at Victoria University. In finishing my last two year's work and attending examinations at Morley I have endured many hardships in the cold weather, ran many risks in swimming rivers on horseback, travelled 2-3,000 miles and expended quite a sum of money in travelling expenses.

'The drill has been good for body, mind and soul and I rejoice that the course is finished and now I can go freely and diligently in studies for some time better adapted to my work for the present as a missionary.'

It always took time to receive answers to his requests for help with funding, with committees having to sit and assess the need. His salary of $850 a year was not large, and initially he was funding the new buildings out of his own salary. What John was unaware of, as it had not been made explicitly clear to him, was that the Missionary Society had little funds even for salaries, let alone capital expenditure for buildings. It was an unwritten rule that missionaries were expected to do the best they could, and if that meant using their own money, then so be it.

Communication was always by letter; indeed, letters were the Maclean's primary link with the outside world, something he lamented in his journal:

'Like angels' visits, letters from friends and family are few and far between, as the mail comes only once a month and when delayed by blizzards does not arrive sometimes for six weeks.

'The monotony and isolation are apt to produce depression of spirits but despite Annie's poor health, never a murmur escapes her lips, though the silent tear is eloquent in a moment of weakness.

'The railroads are coming but we have had to travel on the open prairie in the harshest two winters just gone. When the thermometer was well below zero, we have been stranded in wind and snow and had to throw the tent over the wagon at night, as the ground was too hard to drive the picket pins into the soil. We were awakened by the howling of the storm to find the snow piled up around us.

'Annie is stout and resolute in character but petite in physique and may require some convalescence at home in Guelph to shake off persistent illness.'

This decision was precipitated by the arrival of a letter. It was always with huge excitement that personal missives were received. The couple would re-read letters again and again to fully digest them, celebrating the initial reading with pomp and ceremony. The letter would be saved until the evening, after dinner. A pot of tea would be made, and John and Annie would settle themselves, ready to savour the news from home. They used to take it in turns to read new letters, but John much preferred his wife's recitations, as she invested all of her creativity delivering what was between the lines.

It was normally Olive, the eldest sister, who would write. She had a way with words. Heather and Doris were not as sharp with their observations, nor as cutting with their wit, and feeling that they suffered by comparison, would only write under duress.

'My dearest Annie & John, I hope this letter finds you in better health than when you last wrote to me, sister. If you will, I have a suggestion that might help remedy matters in this respect, but more of that later in this communication, which I am pleased to say is filled with good news.'

Annie grinned, fanning herself with the letter as though to cool herself down.

'Let us guess what the news is, John, come on. Is someone preparing to visit us? Is father retiring and taking mother on a vacation? Even... even... Doris may have become betrothed! Olive mentioned she was courting another teacher. Which do you think, darling? Perhaps something else? At least venture a thought.'

John smiled, delighting in the excitement a letter could bring.

'You are indeed my darling, but I do not have the imagination to wonder about such things. Needless to say, I get as much pleasure from your oration as I do from the content. Pray, read on, for we have had but two sentences and I would like to hear all that has been written before midnight.'

Annie went to swipe at her husband but remembered the letter in her hand. It was far too valuable to risk damaging. She regained her poise before continuing:

'You well remember Emily Stowe, our doctor. The Toronto Women's Literary Club that she helped form has been renamed The Toronto Women's Suffrage Society, and they have petitioned so effectively for improved working conditions for women, and for Toronto schools to accept women in higher education, that it seems a medical college for women in Ontario is finally going to open. Hallelujah!

'Her family are the pioneers, for Emily's daughter, Augusta, has just become the first woman to graduate from the Toronto Medical School. Where she leads others will surely follow. However, I fear it may be too late for me to study. I will explain in a moment.'

'What does she mean, John? What is Olive intimating? Surely... surely, Olive cannot have a romantic attachment also?'

Annie could barely suppress the excitement bubbling inside her. John gestured as though patting an excitable puppy. Yet really there was a part of him that didn't care a jot if his wife got carried away with her conjectures. Her dramatising of every sentence was the only theatre to be experienced for miles around. So, play on.

'Having written about our community, which despite the value of your mission still mourns the loss of you both, I will get down to family matters, which, no doubt, you are keen to hear about.

'I hold you responsible, Annie. It is all your fault...' Annie shot her husband a look of worry, which he batted away nonchalantly with a flick of the wrist and a smile. He was beginning to realise what the news was.

'There we were, four sisters living in perfect harmony within a loving family household. The conversations were – how shall I put it? – healthy and challenging. Which is a polite way of saying, I know we argued but always in good spirit. We all had opinions and were encouraged to air them by our parents, who, despite bemoaning the lack of suitors for their daughters, loved the convivial atmosphere, especially at mealtimes.

'The longer we remained spinsters – I do loathe that word, for it is so judgemental, but for want of a better expression I will use it – the easier it was to avoid questions about marriage, for we had strength in numbers. Our chain was, as the saying goes, only as strong as its weakest link, so when you, Annie, succumbed to the obvious charms of your Scotsman, you put us all at risk.

'What I am trying to say, in my convoluted way, is that we are all to be wed!'

Annie burst into tears and ran into John's arms, squeezing as tightly as her small frame would allow. She babbled away, trying to make herself understood between sobs, then, overcome by excitement, paced the room trying to gather her senses. John, handing her a handkerchief, offered to continue reading the letter but was instantly rebuked:

'I shall get this page framed, for it has in one moment brought me more happiness than the sum of all my years. Aside from your proposal, of course, which wasn't a proposal at all, merely a statement that you were going west and a look that asked me to join you.'

John didn't even try to defend himself on that one, so Annie continued to read:

'Father calls you his "little domino" now, because, despite the fact it is years since you got married, you were the spur that made us all fall in succession.

'Seeing you and John tie the knot was a point of reflection for us all, but it is one thing agreeing to consider taking a husband, quite another finding someone who fits all the criteria.

'Doris is to marry Henry, a teacher with the charisma of a pencil, but they dote on each other and will undoubtedly be very happy. Heather is to marry Arthur, one of Henry's colleagues, who is clearly not suited to teaching; in fact he's not suited to anything at all, apart from his saving grace – he is very funny.

'I, obviously, have made by far the best choice. Men in their twenties are mostly tiresome, and by their thirties they have calmed down and realised that what is in a woman's cranium is more important than what's in the corsage. Fortunately, Cecil is attracted to what's in both. How he is not married I don't know. Early thirties, desperately good looking and the first man I have met who has the same moral clarity as your husband...'

Annie interrupted her own flow to make a point. 'I have always told you that had we not worked out, John, Olive was next in line. She had a soft spot for you.'

John shook his head, smiling bashfully. 'You and I were meant to be from the start. Nothing will ever change that.'

Annie swooned a little before resuming.

'Needless to say I could go on and on about all three men, but you would have to wait 'til summer to get this letter. So, to the point – we want you here for the weddings. We would like both of you, but realise that may be an impossibility; however, we simply cannot get married without you, Annie.

'Pardon me, for my thoughts are getting carried away without due diligence for the practicalities – we are all to be married together. All of our proposals came within a few months of each other, in the spring, and so it made sense to combine the celebrations. We need you as maid of honour to us all.

'Let us assume John cannot venture back for the time being – he could bring you to Minnesota, which is roughly halfway, or a place of your choosing, where father would meet you. You could come home at the tail-end of summer, when the weddings are scheduled, and we will feed you well, you will sleep in a warm bed and you will recover your strengths to return to John when you are fit again. Now what do you both say? Give it some thought and reply in only one way – the affirmative. As ever, your loving sister, Olive.'

Annie flopped back down in her chair, exhausted. John seized his moment.

'Sweetheart, this has been on my mind for some time, and I'm not talking about your sisters, I am talking about a period of convalescence for you. Olive is quite correct about you going home to regain your health.

During that time I can concentrate on building our home and the schools on the reserve.

By the time your recovery is complete, you could return to the reserve, not Fort Macleod, think of that. Then we will be ready to start a family, for we would be foolish to attempt it with you constantly under the weather.

'The letter merely adds to this rationale, and before you attempt to find reasons not to go, save your energy, for I can see in your eyes you know I speak the truth. You also know I can't join you.'

Annie folded into her husband's arms, which had become toned and muscular from the chopping of logs. She shed tears of joy, of sorrow, but mostly tears of love for this man, who felt like a colossus to her.

They sat down, Annie in his lap, nestling her face into his neck and broad shoulders. He enveloped her. It was the feeling she most cherished. She felt inside his love, completely surrounded by it, supported by it and held up by it. How would she survive without it? She wasn't sure, but she did know her husband was right in every respect.

Three months later, the Macleans were on their way to meet Richard, Annie's father, as John recorded:

'We started from the reserve for Blackfoot Crossing, 100 miles distant. When we arrived there, the Canadian Pacific Railroad was within ten miles east of the Crossing. Sickness kept us three days there, and when we were ready for the journey by rail, we had to travel six miles west to reach the construction train, as remarkably the track had been built that distance during our stay.

'All through Sunday, the men worked hard laying rails and it was a strange sight to see the large number of men laying so easily upon the prairie the iron way, keenly watched by the aborigines who pondered deeply upon the white man's skill in being able to make the "fire wagon", as they called it, travel faster that the fastest horse of the red man.

'We had to pay on the construction train for riding in a caboose, which was crowded, the snug sum of eight cents per mile until we reached Medicine Hat. Then, a colonist car was provided, for which we had to pay first class fare until we reached Moose Jaw, where we enjoyed the luxury of a first class carriage but with definite instructions enforced not to turn the seats. By the time we reached our destination we were worn out for the want of sleep, as it was impossible for us to lie down since we left Blackfoot Crossing.'

There was an emotional meeting between Annie and her father, before an evening meal where John was merely a spectator. Annie quizzed Richard on his opinions of the grooms-to-be, and he was unerringly loyal and steadfast.

The following morning, after a brief breakfast, Richard whisked his daughter off on their journey home, anxious to avoid a tortured goodbye. The reverend waved to them both, knowing life would get harder before it got easier without his wife by his side – and how long for?

On John's return trip, at Medicine Hat he met two Blackfoot chiefs on their way to see Lieutenant Governor Dewdney, the man who ran the region on behalf of the government. A dangerous fever had spread amongst the tribes, and at least seventy-five had died within a mere few days, with many more sick besides.

The Blackfoot had ascribed their malaise to the proximity of the whites. 'They'd had too much church' was how one chief put it. The other chief said their sickness was brought about by the arrival of the Canadian Pacific Railway (CPR), and they were determined to tear up the rails. John decided to go with them to see if he could help.

In what was a combustible atmosphere, Father Albert Lacombe did a lot to restore Maclean's faith in the Roman Catholic Church, which had suffered because of the antagonism between himself and Father Trivett. Lacombe distributed tea, sugar, flour and tobacco amongst the troubled congregation, and did much to placate them, holding a council meeting with Governor Dewdney and Chief Crowfoot, 'Chief of Chiefs' as he was also known.

Whether it was because of sickness or encroachment onto reserve territory, there was much suspicion from the chiefs, and only the persuasiveness of Lacombe, Dewdney and Crowfoot assuaged them, allowing the laying of track to continue.

Once back at home, the reverend threw himself into the preparation of his dwelling and the schools on the reserve. It was heavy physical work during the day, and in the evenings strain of another kind, as he immersed himself in writing and study. The latter would lead to a Master of Arts Degree from Victoria University in 1887 and a PhD in Church History from Wesleyan University, Bloomington, Illinois in 1888.

When he wasn't building, much of Maclean's pastoral work involved tending to the sick. He would see between twenty to thirty patients a day, administering medicines and ointments despite his lack of medical training. There was a white doctor at Fort Macleod, but the aborigines preferred to trust a 'praying man', who was more like their own medicine man. He diagnosed the common symptoms as 'biliousness, consumption, running sores, ulcers, worms, coughs and rheumatics'. This work gave the reverend the opportunity to exercise his ever improving grasp of the Blackfoot language.

On one such visit to the Scabby Bull band, as he approached the lodges, Maclean sensed something was wrong. He could see people moving agitatedly between the tipis, and he could hear shouts and loud voices. There was a mêlée around the chief's lodge, and as he approached, Bull Shield was brought out by his principle wife and another man. He looked in a bad way.

It transpired that Bull Shield had never fully got over the death of Siochki, his eight-year-old son. That morning, he had sent everyone in his tipi on an errand of some sort before rigging up a rope and trying to hang himself.

His wife had suspected something untoward and had returned much sooner than expected and before Bull Shield was dead. She had screamed and cut him down. Physically, the chief would be all right, but his depression was shared by many of the people on the reserve.

The reverend counselled him, trying to understand his situation and speaking to him with increasing confidence in Algonkian. He told him of the sadnesses in his own life and the death of his mother when he was young. He explained he had found salvation in God. Bull Shield appreciated the young missionary's efforts but explained that he was not ready to leave his own god, the Great Spirit, who had served him well. It was a refrain the reverend had heard many times.

Looking around the tipi, John saw two buffalo hunting scenes beautifully painted on animal hide. Maclean commented on them to Bull Shield, remarking how important they had been for him in learning about Blackfoot ways. As indigenous people didn't write, they had developed other ways of recording their history – through storytelling, pictures, sign language and other forms of telegraphy.

As a result of his further studies, the reverend was developing a scientific interest in Blackfoot culture and was systematically surveying the ethnographic literature. He asked Bull Shield to help him. By doing this, the chief would not only be helping Maclean, but preserving the traditions so precious to him. It did the trick, giving Bull Shield a sense of purpose on his road back to recovery.

The chief taught the reverend the Blood signs for the fifteen tribes, as well as the sign for the white man, which John particularly liked for its simplicity, recording it in his journal thus:

'Draw the right hand across the forehead with the palm downward and thumb toward the face, which evokes the image of a brimmed hat'.

Bull Shield lived for many more years, before eventually going blind, which put an end to his painting, and he always thanked John for giving him back his pride. Maclean, meanwhile, was able to put what he had learned from the chief to good use, in particular when treating a Blood called Kootenay, who had three shot balls in his body after fighting the Sioux. The two became friends, and when Kootenay became deaf as a result of his wounds, Maclean communicated with him through sign language.

But try as he might, Maclean could not befriend every Blood that he met. He was still a white man in their reserve, and since his arrival he had seen for himself the economic and psychological deterioration of the tribe.

'They have said over and over again "that white men have taken our land, they abuse us when we go to the towns, diseases have been introduced amongst us, so that our chiefs, warriors and young men are dying.

' "A few years ago the land, rivers and trees were ours, but now the white men have fenced in the land, prevented us getting wood, given us whiskey which kills our people, cheated us in trading and they hate us." '

It was against this backdrop, whilst his wife was still in Guelph, that Maclean finally moved into his Mission House. He described the premises as consisting of 'a main house – really a shanty with a mud roof – a fifteen-foot square store room next door to it. A few steps away is a workshop fifteen x eighteen feet and a chicken house fourteen feet square.' It was hardly a palace, but it would suffice. Now he just wanted his wife back by his side in the house he had made for them both.

Chapter Ten

John had waved goodbye to Annie in the middle of summer and hadn't expected to see her for about eight to nine months. The plan was for her to winter at home and return in early spring. He wasn't to know that Annie was already pregnant with their first son. When she wrote to tell him, John had to sit down.

In one sense he was overjoyed, but in another he was frustrated at not being with his wife to support her through her pregnancy. But the more he thought about it, the more he realised it was for the best.

In Guelph, she would be looked after, attended to, well fed, and would have medical help should she need it. A birth either in Macleod or on the reserve would have been fraught with potential difficulties. It was in everyone's best interests that Annie was at her parent's house.

Annie wrote every month to sustain and fortify John, and he relied upon these letters to keep his spirits high. Ordinarily, naming their child might have filled multiple letters, but they had already decided that if it was a boy he would be christened Richard, and if it was a girl she would be Alice.

Before Annie's return, Maclean held his first service for the Bloods on their reserve, where he spoke to them in their language and read his own translation of three verses of the first chapter of John's Gospel. After this, he sang his redoubtable favourite, 'Jesus, Lover of My Soul'. The First Nations people thought it touching that a white man should get so emotionally involved when singing a hymn; they of course did not know how much the words meant to him.

The reverend had missed his wife more than he cared to admit, and on their reunion in Minnesota, he was overjoyed to see the sparkle in her eye and the pride with which she showed off their son. Annie and Richie, which is how she introduced her son to her husband, both looked a picture of health and happiness, ready to launch themselves into the next phase of their life together on the reserve.

As he travelled back, holding his son, John was completely enamoured by his plump, ruddy cheeks and could not believe how much he slept. His repose gave Annie the opportunity to give full vent to what she really wanted to talk about – her sisters.

Having been starved of their company for so long, during her year at home she had over indulged and now needed to offload all the emotional baggage taken on board. She went into almost encyclopaedic depth about the wedding, the grooms and the relationships, but was rather perturbed that John was not asking any questions of her.

John replied that he was mesmerised by Richie, and although enchanted by her recollections, nowhere was there any facet of what she had said that he could unpick or unravel. She had simply covered everything. Annie wasn't sure if that was a veiled but playful insult, which of course it was, but it mattered not. They were now a family.

Once home, John picked up his wife and child to carry them over the threshold of their shanty. Annie's reaction was in marked contrast to when they had first arrived in Fort Macleod, when she had been secretly devastated to discover their primitive living quarters in town. Her expectations were now different, her resolve strengthened, and she knew what she was walking into. They much preferred the reserve to Macleod, and settled in straight away, feeling closer to nature and much more independent.

The First Nations they lived closest to welcomed them, but they still resented the general encroachment of the white man, and acceptance was not universal further afield. John was always aware of this fact and monitored the mood of the people he administered to. But children are marvellous brokers of peace, and Richie's presence undoubtedly helped the Macleans' integration into indigenous society, for it indicated the missionary's trust in them.

After a year or so, Annie fell pregnant again. It was happy news, but the political situation in Canada was changing, giving the Macleans cause to worry when the North-West Rebellion started in March 1885.

The Métis were a race born out of the growth of Canada's fur trade, which had expanded westwards from the 1600s. They originated from the French Canadian fur traders who married or lived with mainly

Cree, Ojibwa or Saulteaux women, with their offspring being called 'Métis', meaning 'people of mixed blood'.

They were a distinct group of Canadians with a proud culture and rich heritage, combining elements of both peoples from which they descended. They were excellent riders and marksmen, and wore moccasins and a distinctive red sash across their torso. They loved to meet and dance, invariably to the sound of the fiddle, and were devout Catholics, with a language that was a mixture of French and Cree.

The Métis believed that Canada had failed to protect their rights, their land and their survival as a specific group of people. Louis Riel led the Métis, along with some Cree and Assiniboines, in a brief and unsuccessful uprising. Maclean supported their argument but, as it turned into a military action, not their application of it:

'Preached last Sunday at Pincher Creek to a large congregation. People excited all over the country through the Riel Rebellion at Prince Albert. Two police and twelve citizens on government side killed – intense enthusiasm in Canada. People at Macleod very much excited. They are afraid the Bloods will rise.

'Have moved my wife to town owing to the exciting influences that have been at work, especially the uneasiness shown amongst the Bloods since the commencement of the Rebellion.'

Maclean continued at the mission, questioning in his journal why the Blackfoot confederacy didn't join the uprising given their dissatisfaction with their own state of affairs. He reasoned the ancient enmity between Blackfoot, Métis and Cree leant a natural distrust of each other – they were hardly natural allies.

A further factor in Blackfoot nonparticipation was, he noted, a consensus of opinion amongst the Blackfoot head chiefs that his friend Red Crow had played a leading part in forming: 'The old men are loyal to the Government and Mékaisto [Red Crow] is, by nature, a man of peace'.

The other leading chief, Crowfoot, believed entering the rebellion would not be in his people's best interests.

Maclean remained steadfast too. He was a watchful observer on the edge of the reserve and an active advocate for Bloods' maintaining the peace. He sent periodic reports to the police headquarters at Fort Macleod, and he had Red Crow's assurances of personal safety. He was not the only missionary who stayed in position, and their steadfastness helped to reassure the First Nations that there were some white men who supported their cause.

Within a matter of months, the rebellion was over, with the Canadian Pacific Railway, although still unfinished, playing a key role, having allowed the government to mobilise forces far quicker than it had been able to do so in the past. The successful operation increased political support for the floundering and incomplete railway, which had been close to financial collapse, and further funds were authorised to finish the line.

Maclean did not support the hanging of the leaders of the rebellion; he preferred 'severe punishment', without specifying what that would be. He remained unwavering in his conviction that the causes of indigenous unrest needed 'urgent attention', and that the only 'true remedy' would be the institution of special councils, which would include chiefs, government officials, missionaries and teachers.

These councils would listen to aboriginal grievances, report on them and see to their redress. In so doing they would help remedy growing discord by raising the status of the aborigine to that of his counterpart, the white man.

With perfect timing John and Annie's second son was born a month after the rebellion had ended. Their second arrival, Walter, was one of three children born on the reserve, and all of them entered the world in very trying conditions. The third born, Oswald, was delivered 'under the care of a doctor so inebriated be could stand only with difficulty'.

Oswald was called 'Owie' by Walter, and as is the way in families, the name stuck. Their fourth child was a girl, and John honoured his own mother by naming her Alice.

Throughout all the adversity their life entailed, Annie remained constant and brave, and in his journal John reflected on his admiration for the mother of his children:

'Once we were caught on the old north trail in a fearful hail storm with no covering for protection on the wagon. The frightened horses speeding like demons to escape the smarting pain... Annie tucked her garments around her and put her feet high on the dashboard cradling our two children (there was another coming but we were unawares).

'We came to a swollen river and I guided the horses over the bar [an elevated region of sediment] whilst Annie held the reins and our swaddled babes.

'Twenty feet from the bar the rapids fell to a depth

of fifteen feet or so, and there were folks watching on the shore, this dangerous but necessary manoeuvre, who would have been unable to render any assistance should the worst have happened.

'When the prairie fire swept through the coulee [a dry ravine where once water flowed], it was Annie who bundled the children behind the buckboard on the wagon and helped to fight the fire.

'When the call came from a sick woman fifty miles away, though the mountain streams were surging with the melting snows and there were no bridges, Annie went with a strange driver, a man she had never seen before, and though darkness would set in before the end of the trip, she packed her small valise and was off on her mission of mercy.

'After ten days' nursing, she came back with two pounds of butter and two dozen eggs to help eke out the disconsolate larder in the mission house.

'When the parcels of small clothes missed the last winter post from Ontario, one of the tiny Macleans was but six months old. Annie was invariably consumed with mirth when she had to dress her son in red flannel or black and white silk made from her own clothes.

'Then there was the finger which had to be amputated after a severe infection, the well beloved Dr Kennedy of Macleod who had replaced his drunken predecessor, did all he could to save it but to no avail.

'Acting as his own anaesthetist, he removed it – the middle finger of the right hand. With a four months old baby and three small children and no help available, Annie, the brave little mother suffered and fought it out.

'When I went to Edmonton, which was two or three

times a year, I was absent five weeks each time and Annie was left alone among the aborigines with our children and their friends to care for; however, never a murmur escaped her lips.'

As well as the trips to Edmonton, Maclean was still travelling to Morley to deliver papers he had prepared for his MA and subsequent doctorate. John McDougall, his immediate boss, was based in Morley, and perhaps because the reverend was always coming to him, he felt no compulsion to go and see him on the reserve. This would cause resentment between the pair at the end of the decade, by which time McDougall had only visited the man he had chosen for the job three times over ten years.

Whilst in Morley, John would always catch up with George Maclean, who was now managing to harness his temper and channel it into productive study. The only problem was the draw of the wild. Walking Buffalo would often do exactly that – walk, not to mention run, jump and swim in the land he regarded as his home, before returning to school a few days later.

The reverend recorded:

'George has ability. He could be a minister of the gospel, a medical doctor or anything you can name if he would stay in school. That's the problem – keeping him in school.

'I propose we send Tatanga Mani to St John's College in Winnipeg. He couldn't run away from there so easily and it would be a useful experiment to place an indigenous boy in school with white boys. We'd all be proud if he came back with a diploma or degree, ready to serve his own people. And if the test proves to be a success we can send more young aborigines.'

As always Maclean ran the idea past John McDougall, who thought, if George and his family were receptive to the idea, it was worth a try.

While Winnipeg was a long way away, the Anglican school had an excellent reputation and was one of the oldest schools in the country. But when Maclean and McDougall presented the proposition, Walking Buffalo was unimpressed. He felt sure he would be better off settling down to life on the reservation, where he could live like a First Nation. But the two men persisted, both believing it was in George's best interests to get as good an education as possible.

They asked him which he would rather be, a missionary to his people or a medical doctor working amongst them. George preferred the notion of a medical doctor, and McDougall promised to help find the money to take him to St John's College School, provided he would work at it.

McDougall elaborated: 'It will take quite a few years of study, but imagine how much good you could do for the Stonies if you came back as a trained doctor. Your people could quit using herbs, quit this brewing of chokecherry bark to cure coughs and colds, this boiling of seneca root to get a laxative. These medicines might be better than nothing, but a real doctor would be a great improvement.'

Chief Bearspaw of the Stonies and George's father, Wolf Ear, gave their reluctant permission, and a few months later Walking Buffalo boarded a train for Winnipeg from Morley. He was slightly put out that none of the white people on board the 'iron horse' wanted to speak with a young aborigine boy. So he took to staring out of the window, his flat nose pressed hard against the glass.

As he left the mountains and foothills behind, Walking Buffalo felt alone and uncertain, but he was determined to make a go of things. The train rocked along, and his mind started to wander. East of Calgary, he tried to imagine the now bare prairies filled with thousands of buffaloes as in days gone by. Then they passed through Gleichen, renowned as Blackfoot country, followed by the Cree territory of Maple Creek and Regina. Finally the conductor announced they were in Manitoba, and George knew he was passing across soil that, in years gone by, Assiniboines, Sioux and Cree had battled over.

Winnipeg was strange, with more people than he had ever encountered. Two roads, Main Street and Portage Avenue, had this weird block paving, but all the others seemed to be this unusually sticky mud. Street cars operated on rails and were hauled by single horses, but there were also fine carriages and horse-drawn vehicles moving about the streets like milling cattle. There seemed to be no rules, with whoever was bolder going first.

In Winnipeg, Walking Buffalo was met by a teacher who took him up to the school, where he felt daunted by the size of the building. His school in Morley was a one-room log shack. The brick and stone edifice he now looked at seemed a million miles away from the peacefulness of the Bow River and the Rocky Mountains.

He was then introduced to Anthony, the boy he was to room with. When they were alone for the first time, and Walking Buffalo was unpacking his clothes, Anthony asked him, 'Did you bring your bow and arrows with you?' From that point on, Anthony did not hide his resentment at being paired with an aborigine.

George's first day of classes was a mystery to him. He was uninspired and mystified by the lessons, but at least the teachers were kind. The meals were good and his bed was 'softer than a buffalo robe thrown on the ground'.

On those first few lonely nights, Tatanga Mani pined for his home like never before. If he'd had a bag of moccasins, he'd have set off on foot for his homeland, which was a thousand miles west of Winnipeg. But a teacher spoke encouragingly to him and assured him that things would get easier. And they did.

He started to see the point of reading, writing and arithmetic. His confidence was improving, and he started to socialise. Not all white boys were like Anthony. George had a ready smile, athletic gait and a keen sense of humour, which meant he was soon accepted.

He also soon gained his room-mate's respect and thanks, when Anthony took a canoe for a paddle on the ice swollen Red River in April and got into real difficulties when he capsized. It was George who plunged into the 'Muddy Red' to save him, causing Anthony to apologise for his prejudiced behaviour. In time, the two pupils became firm friends.

In his tipi, Chief Bearspaw nodded sagely as George read the principal's report, which outlined 'Maclean's great potential... ability to learn quickly... abundant personal qualities that mean he gets on well with so many boys', describing him as 'someone who has made a real impact in the school'.

The chief was impressed, glad that an indigenous boy had succeeded in a white boy's school. But he was also worried. He felt the Stonies needed someone who could bridge the ever-widening gap between honoured aboriginal customs and the fast-moving world of the white man. Though he had no idea what their future would look like, he knew that a transition into some sort of integrated society was essential for the tribe's survival. Only strong leadership would make it happen, and that leadership would have to come from someone who personified what a good aboriginal could be. Namely, someone in tune with nature who valued the environment, respected the land and supported everyone in their community. Bearspaw felt Walking Buffalo had those qualities.

Here was a strong and thoughtful young man able to read and write and hold his own amongst white boys. He oozed confidence, seemingly never overawed by the world of the white man. The chief looked on Tatanga Mani almost as a son and feared he would be lured away to work and live in the towns and cities.

It was a hugely important time, not only for the Stoney tribe but for all aboriginal people, and the chief wanted Walking Buffalo at the core of moving them forward with the times. They needed Tatanga Mani more than he needed them, but in time that might change too. Although he didn't say this directly to him, Bearspaw didn't want George to go back to school. He would work on him during the summer and early autumn before his return to Winnipeg.

Shortly after this, Bearspaw received an invitation from the Agricultural Society in the rapidly growing town of Calgary forty-five miles away. The society had decided to invite the Sarcee and Stoney Indians to a new initiative, the Calgary Fair (later to become the Calgary Stampede). Bearspaw thought sending a representation of his people would be a good gesture, and he wanted Walking Buffalo in the party. 'You'd better go,' he said to the young man. 'Your eyes are open. You'll see everything and you'll learn something if you go. Then you can tell me what you think about it all.'

Along with eight other Stonies, Walking Buffalo sat in the horse-drawn wagon from which tent poles fanned out like a magpie's tail feathers. A couple of yellow dogs followed faithfully. Once in open country, the white bones of buffalo were evident in the grass, now sadly a relic of a bygone era, and as they neared Calgary, hawks cut circles against the clear sky, hovering above the town that had grown up around the Mounted Police fort established over a decade before.

The Stonies were invited to pitch their tipis right in the centre of town, but they preferred not to be one of the attractions and instead decided to camp next to the Bow River, as they had done for generations past when hunting.

Walking Buffalo didn't know it at the time, but his attendance at the first Calgary Fair would be an annual pilgrimage for the next eighty years. On their return, he spoke to Bearspaw about what he had seen:

'The white people thought we were just there for their entertainment, but they overlooked something.

They didn't guess that we were watching them just as much as they were watching us.

'I know many white people who act so wisely, but many I saw at the fair seemed practically strangers to the ways of nature and consumed with competitiveness about bizarre matters.

'We found it difficult to understand why it mattered if one man had bigger potatoes or better wheat or healthier cows, and yet they were showing off their possessions to determine who owned the best.

'Their urge to surpass all others accounts for white men's drive and hurried behaviour. I feel sorry for them. They disregard nature for what it is and all the gifts it has to offer.

'This is the fundamental difference between them and us. We have always lived a communal way of life. Cooperation is essential for survival, so we live as equals as for generations past.

'We must learn to get on with the competitive white man, and to do that we must understand him so we can find common ground. But this works both ways, and he must make an effort to understand our ways too. This was a good start. Not only that, we got free beef and I returned a prize-winner. Without telling me, the McDougalls entered some mitts I had made into the leather glove section, and I won first prize.'

Bearspaw recognised that his young charge spoke with a wisdom beyond his years. He thought it only right to tell him of his hopes and fears. Walking Buffalo felt greatly honoured to be thought of in such glowing terms, but felt in a quandary about what he should do.

He sought the counsel of his father, Wolf Ear,

listened to his grandmothers, and then consulted with the two missionaries, McDougall and Maclean. Both the churchmen felt it would be a waste not to finish his studies when he had already achieved so much, but the groundswell of opinion amongst his biological family convinced him he was needed on the reservation, where Chief Bearspaw still held ultimate sway. It was decided Walking Buffalo would stay and serve as an interpreter for his people. But with his formal education now over, his future was as uncertain as the mountain weather.

John returned to Annie to tell her of their adopted son's decision. The reverend couldn't hide his disappointment. As he saw it, education was the key to indigenous social integration, and he thought that, had he pursued his studies, George would have made an excellent role model to younger Stonies. Annie balanced this perspective by outlining the needs of Walking Buffalo's tribe. Her husband understood and valued what she said, just as he respected Bearspaw's rationale for wanting George on the reservation. Yet still he disagreed. Personal betterment, John thought, would have led to greater individual achievement for Walking Buffalo and resulted in larger collective gain for the Stonies.

Chapter Eleven

John's own betterment continued apace in the second half of the 1880s. The advent, in quick succession, of three children into the mission house could have seriously curtailed his studies for his MA and PhD, but he was fortunate that all of their children slept well, enabling him to study during the evenings.

For Richie, Walter, Owie and latterly Alice, life on the reserve could not have been more active. They were fully accepted by Button Chief's band of Bloods, as if they were their own blood. They played amongst the tipis and roamed and foraged with the older children, always with Annie not far behind.

The women were amused how much Annie worried about her children. Indigenous women learnt to trust older siblings and friends to take the lead in exploratory play. This, they said, led to independent minds and people with confidence among the land they lived in.

Annie was able to laugh at herself in this respect, but still she found it hard to let go of the ideas of her own upbringing, within the confines of a building and a fenced off garden. On the reserve, there were no real boundaries apart from the river, and children learned very quickly about the laws of nature and how to respect them.

As soon as the young Macleans could walk, they were up and running with the pack, leading gloriously energetic lives based on practical skills. They discovered berries you could eat, plants you shouldn't touch, animals to beware of, and when they were of a certain age, how to build a fire and light it safely.

Annie played her part too. Not only were her children learning to speak English, but also Algonkian, and she helped their friends develop bilingually as well. The children could not have been happier; neither could they have been more engaged with their environment.

Annie thrived in the communal spirit of the reserve. She loved the concept that everyone lived solely off the land, which they didn't consider they owned, simply looked after for their children. They lived sustainably, doing no harm to it and protecting their resources. When animals were caught, everything was used, with wasted meat almost considered a crime, dishonouring the animal and the hunter who had caught it.

Annie learnt to make jerky, cutting the meat into thin strips and drying it in the sun, and pemmican too. The latter was made of dried meat ground into a powder, with just enough fat to make it stick together and dried berries added to give it some flavour. Then it was rolled into balls or cut into strips. Pemmican seemed to last forever, and Annie wanted to ensure John had sustenance on his trips around the reserve.

Of her three sons, Richie was the one who really blossomed in his open-air classroom. He was small-framed like his mother but had his father's musculature, making him very nimble and athletic. He and his friends played hide-and-seek in the forest, which was how they learnt the necessary skills of tracking animals and attacking enemy tribes.

He was taught the Fox Walk, which was designed to help you walk as silently as the wily creature. You took part barefoot or with moccasins, so that you had a feel for what you were stepping on, avoiding twigs that might give your position away. Your heel had to strike the ground in a very controlled manner, and then you had to push your weight onto the ball of your foot, reducing your footprint and noise. If you were travelling with someone, they placed their foot directly in your footprint. It was a slow and methodical way of travelling that preserved your energy and allowed you to move quietly.

Richie was light on his feet and had an acute sense of balance, enabling him to stand on one leg and hold his position until he was ready to move. His peers lauded him for the speed with which he picked up these tracking skills. He would show his brothers what he had learnt, and Annie loved watching her 'three little foxes' striding around outside the mission house, some more wobbly than others.

Such were his skills that Richie was given the name of Pale Fox. He loved it, but it led to his brothers' wanting names too. Annie spoke to her women friends, who gladly christened Walter as Snow Owl, because he had had little hair for his first two years but when it came it was blonde and thick, like the plumage of the bird. His protruding ears also gave him excellent hearing, something it was revered for. Owie was called Little Coyote, because in his early months he had a cry that mimicked a pup's call for milk.

When Alice arrived, it was Richie who inadvertently gave her a name. Their father led the three boys in to see their proud mother, who had just given birth to the daughter she had craved. Annie was tired but exultant as her sons approached the bed.

John introduced them to their sister, and Richie remarked that she looked like an animal he'd held a few days earlier in the forest – a pygmy shrew.

Annie shook her head and laughed.

'My daughter looks like a pygmy shrew! Oh my goodness.'

Richie explained, 'Well, a pygmy shrew is tiny and very pretty, and they have small pointy noses like Alice.'

Thankfully, Annie liked the analogy.

'In which case, you have just given your sister her indigenous name of Pygmy Shrew. What do you think of that, Owie? Can you say that name?'

Owie, whose own name had metamorphosed already, was just over a year old, and Annie was keen to develop his speech, which can be slower with bilingual children. He tried to frame the words 'pygmy shrew' but what came out instead was 'Peggy-Sue'.

Everyone laughed, except John, whose hands came up to smack his forehead. For years he had dreamt of giving a daughter the name of his mother, whose memory he still cherished. But as his hands lowered slowly from his face, he smiled, for as he surveyed their bedroom, with all they had created, he realised he had so much to be thankful for.

Owie toddled along the edge of the bed, chanting 'Peggy-Sue! Peggy-Sue! Peggy-Sue!' He wouldn't stop until his brothers ceased laughing. John sighed in a mock-melancholy way, knowing what was done was done.

'No matter what you scoundrels call your sister I shall call her "Alice",' he said.

He embraced his wife then ushered his sons out of their bedroom. Annie needed to suckle Alice and then to get some rest.

John took his sons to go and make a shelter on the edge of a small woodland, one of their favourite past-times. He would have to take a few days off his missionary activities until Annie was sufficiently recovered, although she had been remarkably quick to resume her maternal role when her boys had been born.

John's own survival skills had developed out of necessity. By his own admission, when he had started traversing the Blackfoot reserve, he had been like a fish out of water. But as his grasp of the language improved, he could better listen to the natives' advice, and he learnt quickly, writing down what he was told.

Button Chief ensured that, if he didn't instruct the reverend directly, someone he trusted did. His first principle of survival was to foster a tight-knit community that looked after its own. Within his band, as in many others, everyone helped each other, sharing their specialties to forge a strong collective.

The second principle seemed strange to Maclean, but he soon found it to be true. Button Chief was adamant that survival was a spiritual quest and therefore involved creating works of art. Survival was the art in question, and the time, energy and care that went into ensuring each tool's utmost efficiency and utility were the artistry. He explained that techniques essential to staying alive were passed down from generation to generation. Accordingly, layer upon layer, these techniques were honoured, acquired, refined when necessary, and became part of the tradition of the tribe.

The reverend found that if he made shelters with this attitude in mind, he made them better, keeping him and his boys drier and warmer. It gave him a new level of respect for the artfulness of wilderness living.

John's family life gave him huge fulfilment and welcome relief from the stresses and strains of maintaining the mission, which he found depressing at times. His concerns were manifold, and his worries about the social situation of the Bloods were only increasing:

'The present condition of the people is in striking contrast with that of the time when first I saw them. Then, they had buffalo-skin lodges and buffalo robes which they used as blankets.

'Many of them had beautiful deerskin shirts nicely ornamented with beadwork but that is now all gone. Many of them come to the mission house poorly clad, asking for clothing to cover their nakedness and protect them from the severity of the weather.

'I received a pair of moccasins for one of my little boys from a woman I engaged to make them as I am too busy to afford the time to make them myself. After paying her the sum agreed upon, she begged for presents as a token of friendship. This custom they learned from trading with the whiskey traders who sold them inferior goods at high rates and then gave them presents.'

Health remained a key issue. Word had reached Maclean of a smallpox epidemic in Montréal that had killed close to six thousand people. A similar outbreak amongst the Bloods would wipe them out completely.

In the decade since the signing of Treaty Seven and with the disappearance of the buffalo, Maclean had seen an appreciable decline in the quality of life of the Bloods. Their diet was poor, and fighting infection was increasingly difficult. Annual mortality rates were officially at about ten per cent, but the reverend felt this might be a conservative estimate.

Cattle and horse stealing were still rife, polygamy the norm. The Missionary Society was having difficulty attracting teachers to work in the two schools Maclean had built, and when they sent a certain Mr Clipsham, he was found to be totally incompetent. Trying to get rid of him was just another woe added to the reverend's list.

As always, in trying to combat this range of problems, John relied on Annie for guidance and morale. They were now both fluent in Blackfoot and were busy compiling the Blackfoot Grammar and Dictionary. Alongside this work, they were also both collecting and studying the legendary lore of their friends. Their conviction in the worth of these studies was only heightened by their awareness of the changing world of the people they were serving:

'Time is short and we must toil hard, for the Bloods are fast losing their hold upon traditional ways and in a few years these things will have become so greatly changed as to be unrecognisable, if not altogether lost'.

Accordingly, John redoubled his efforts, researching, studying and evaluating the Bloods from an ethnographic standpoint. After his first book had been published in 1882, he had circulated a whole series of pamphlets, articles and papers on First Nation affairs, some of them under a pseudonym because of their politically contentious content. His subsequently acquired Master of Arts degree and doctorate in Church History gave added weight to his arguments. He would soon be the Reverend Doctor John Maclean BA, MA, and was fast gaining a reputation as an indigenous expert.

He began a long-time correspondence with Horatio Hale, an eminent Harvard-educated ethnologist, who enlisted Maclean and Father Lacombe to collect data on the Blackfoot for the British Scientific Association in London. Hale later wrote, 'the most useful contributions which the sciences of ethnology and linguistics have yet received have come from able and devoted missionaries'. Soon after this, John also began exchanging letters with staff members at the Smithsonian Institute in Washington DC, who wanted a collection of objects and documentation as to how they were made and used.

Not to be outdone, the president of the Canadian Institute in Toronto encouraged Maclean to collect artefacts and ethnographic information, whilst Franz Boas of Harvard University, a noted anthropologist, asked the reverend to collect myths and legends for publication.

As Maclean became more and more recognised as

an authority on aboriginal matters, his capacity for work remained rapacious. He became a Public School Inspector in 1886 and a member of the North-West Board of Education two years later.

In the midst of all this, Annie was raising four young children in a mud shanty on a reserve. Yet, for all of John's achievements in a variety of spheres, a dark cloud loomed large on the horizon. It was inescapably ominous, threatening to overshadow all of the reverend's achievements in the near decade he had been a missionary.

It was a simple matter of fact that for all his preaching, all his ministrations, all of his endeavours, John Maclean had not managed to convert one soul to the Methodist cause.

During that time, Annie had bolstered him, convinced him that things would change, but the hour of reckoning was coming and could not be avoided. In one of his weaker moments, John poured scorn on his own lamentable performance, writing,

'My contrition is valid and well-earned for I have toiled long and hard to attract these people to Methodism. Alas, my work seems to have been in vain. Their eyes and ears have received me, more so as I speak in their tongue, but I cannot win over their hearts and souls.

'To think of all the missionaries who have ever deemed to venture forth into the wilderness with the power of God behind them – theirs was an historic era. It pains me to think of myself as an historic failure. Not one soul saved. Not one. Can there ever have been a missionary with such a paltry return after so much effort? I fear not. Woe is me for mine must be the least successful mission that ever was and I the least successful missionary that ever lived.'

John knew that Annie always read through his journal, and he wrote these statements as a sort of confessional. But before she had had the chance to attend to it, he picked up his pen again:

'My recourse is to be found in my family, my studies and in a renewal of my consecration to God as a living sacrifice. In such things I find solace and a feeling of redemption. Dear merciful, loving and compassionate God, unworthy am I to call thee Father, yet to thee I must come, that help for my soul may be given.

'Here I consecrate myself, body, soul and spirit, all I possess, time, talents, riches, wife, children, friends, reputation, all, everything to thee now and forever, unreservedly thine. To live for thee. To labour for thee. To follow thee. Thine I am. Thine I will be.'

Annie would flick through John's writings as she fed Alice. Her daughter was a slow feeder, but Annie was at everyone's beck and call all day, and she loved the intimacy of having Peggy-Sue to herself (against all of John's efforts, the name was there to stay).

Alice's last feed of the day was always after the boys were tucked up in bed. Mother and daughter would look at each other, a moment of serenity that John loved watching from his desk as he worked. Observing his suckling children had become his evening entertainment since the moment Richie had been born. It calmed him, giving him a sense of perspective and keeping him grounded when he began building things up out of all proportion.

But when Annie read what John had written about his sense of failure, her blood began to boil. Alice picked up immediately on her mother's fury, detached herself from her breast and started to cry, more in protest than in distress. Annie thrust their daughter into John's arms and strode about the room in an agitated fashion.

'Oh, John! Self-pity is so unattractive. Where is the man whose strength of character bowled me over? Where is the man, born in Scotland, who had the courage to escape his humble beginnings and fashion a life in Canada, making a man of himself? Where is the person who fulfilled his dream of becoming a missionary, not just to serve God but to help peoples in need? You just don't understand, do you? You don't get it!'

John rose from his desk to place Alice on his chest. Her chin rested delicately on his broad, supportive shoulder as he rubbed her back in a circling motion to wind her. It was the way he had winded all his four 'bairns', as he called them.

'I don't understand. I don't get what?' he asked.

The tiny belch in his ear was a welcome sign that his paternal duties had been successful. Annie got herself comfortable back in her favoured chair and signalled to her husband she was ready to resume her daughter's feed. Cradling the smooth head of the product of their love with his gnarled hand, he passed Alice back to his wife.

She told John to bring a stool so he could sit close to her and they could talk in whispers so as not to disturb Alice. He dutifully obliged, but Peggy-Sue was having none of it. She latched back onto her mother's nipple but kept both eyes wide open. She wanted an amiable resolution and wasn't going to go into a sleepy feed until she had got one.

John shuffled the stool in as close as he could get, his legs splayed, Annie's inside his, their baby cosseted between them. John leant forward and held his wife's free hand. She stroked his palm lovingly.

'Let me explain, my dearest.'

John nodded, anxious to hear Annie's words of wisdom, which were always a source of comfort to him. Her heart rate had reduced, and with great assuredness Annie resumed her exposition:

'Everything the Bloods hold dear to them has changed. The buffalo have gone. Indigenous rituals like the Sun Dance are not allowed. They were nomads roaming free, now they are farmers on a reserve. They used to be fearsome fighters, now they are at peace. Stealing horses, which they saw as a sport, is outlawed.

'And what has the white man given them in return? Treaty Seven, which is no good to man nor beast. Fences they hate. Whiskey they can't handle. Disease they can't control. Government they don't trust. Religions that fight over them. Traders who fleece them. The list goes on and on.

'Taking all of this into consideration, there is one thing, one ever present link with their traditions and customs, that the white man has no influence over – their beliefs.

'The Great Spirit, their god, encapsulates all of their culture. He is their spiritual link with the land, their environment and their old way of life. Is it any wonder they cling on to him?

'Consider the three forces acting upon you: namely, the demands of the Missionary Society, the needs of these aboriginal people, and finally satisfying your own conscience. This triplicity of demands is impossible to fulfil. They all pull in different directions – something had to give. In the first six months of our mission, I knew we were fighting an uphill battle, unable to satisfy these conflicting criteria—'

John interrupted her, 'So why didn't you speak? Say something? Express your concerns?'

'Because I knew it wouldn't make any difference, for the key to the whole matter is, and I've said it before, that these people need us and we meet that need. You respect them, don't force God on them, and in turn, they show respect for you.

'You connect with them, engage with them, speak their language, bury their children, live amongst them, pray with them and try to understand what they are going through at a time of huge cultural change. You have done untold good, and if you think this is failure then give me more of it.

'The Missionary Society wants to effect change too rapidly. Perhaps this is the most contentious part of my argument, but in your heart of hearts, I truly believe you think it is in the Bloods' best interests to maintain their belief in the Great Spirit. At least, for the time being. The natives need a period of consolidation where they can come to terms with everything that has happened to them. We have taken them as far as we can within the confines of our mission.

'So, after nearly a decade of the mission, we are coming to the end. This is a natural impasse. The Society cannot condone funding a mission that does not deliver converts, regardless of the fact that it has underpaid you and not supported you effectively. But the blame is not yours. The society has simply taken on a task too big for the resources at its disposal.

'Yet believe this, in the eyes of God you have acted selflessly. In the lives of our friends you have been nothing other than a positive influence. As far as the Missionary Society is concerned, you have failed, but fear not, for you have had your priorities right all along.'

Annie concluded her discourse by passing Alice to her husband. Their daughter's fight to avoid sleep was over. Now that her parents were calm, she succumbed to the land of nod as John raised her onto his shoulder once more, singing the song he always sung before he placed his children in bed.

It was an old Celtic folk song that his soft voice suited perfectly, but as the original lament was from a male to a female, it felt much more appropriate to be singing it to his daughter:

> *'Oh, the summertime is coming*
> *And the trees are sweetly blooming*
> *And the wild mountain thyme*
> *Grows around the blooming heather.*
> *Will ye go, Lassie, go?*
> *And we'll all go together*
> *To pluck wild mountain thyme*
> *All around the blooming heather.*
> *Will ye go, Lassie, go?*

I will build my love a tower
Near yon' pure crystal fountain
And on it I will build
All the flowers of the mountain.
Will ye go, Lassie, go?

And we'll all go together
To pluck wild mountain thyme
All around the blooming heather.
will ye go, Lassie, go?
If my true love she were gone
I would surely find another
To pluck wild mountain thyme
Grows around the blooming heather. Will ye go, Lassie, go?
And we'll all go together
To pluck wild mountain thyme
All around the blooming heather.
Will ye go, Lassie go?
Let us go, Lassie, go.'

Every rendition stopped Annie in her tracks, sending goose pimples down her spine. No matter how many times she heard it, her body tingled. Familiarity did not breed contempt in any way, shape or form.

Part of John's attraction was his foreignness. Even after all their years of marriage, there was still an unplumbed depth of character. This song only added to the mystique. It transported Annie to the glens and moorland of a land she had heard so much about but knew she was unlikely ever to see.

Her husband hummed it through again as he placed Alice in her bed. They were in meagre surroundings, but

Annie felt that if a person's wealth was judged by the quality of her family, she was a rich woman indeed.

Chapter Twelve

In his role as school's inspector, Maclean was on his way to see what was happening in the school on the Stoney reserve. Word had reached him that Walking Buffalo had become involved in its running, and John wanted to catch up with him. He hadn't been able to visit George since the decision had been taken not to send him back to St John's College. John wondered how the well educated young man had fared back on the reserve.

The first person John met was McDougall, who greeted him in his normal, slightly brusque tone.

'Morning, Maclean! Or should I say Reverend Doctor John Maclean BA, MA. Congratulations! I haven't seen you since your doctorate was conferred. Any news of converts, brother?'

Just before John departed, Annie had warned him of this possible reaction:

'There will be those Methodists envious of your continued academic progress and growing reputation. They will see an irony in the fact that your performance as a converter of these people does not match up.

'That is understandable, but do not let it affect you. Stand tall. Be proud of your achievements. Besides, some bands are canny. They have "belonged" to a number of churches, receiving clothes, food and church relics before reverting to the Great Spirit once the missionary's back is turned. Who can blame them?'

Maclean had undeniable respect for McDougall, despite their friendship having been tested a number of times over the decade. But he knew his boss' compliment was barbed with inherent criticism. He chose not to take the bait. McDougall had been pulled from his studies early by his father, and had not had the wherewithal to complete his degree. As such, he had a begrudging respect for his protégé's commitment and motivation.

During the journey, John had come to terms with Annie's evaluation of their mission, realising it was now only a matter of time before they moved on, whether of their own volition or by order of the Missionary Society.

A benign smile broke John's lips as McDougall shook him by the hand.

'George will be pleased to see you, Maclean,' the older man said. 'He has been awaiting your arrival with some anticipation, it must be said. You'll find him in the school house. Go, I have things to arrange.'

John felt he was only getting half the story, but in his compliant way, he did as he was told. All heads turned as the reverend opened the school house door, where a man, Mr White, was teaching and George was helping a small group of young pupils with their work.

George smiled broadly at the sight of his adoptive father, giving added weight to the conspiracy theory forming in the reverend's mind. The feeling only increased when George whispered something to a young boy, who scurried away. The teacher thanked George for his help and then ushered him and the reverend out of school.

Walking Buffalo always called his adoptive father by his first name, as a mark of respect to his biological father, Wolf Ear.

'Let us go for a walk, John,' he said now. 'I have much to tell you. I could only wait another week for you, otherwise I would have had to go ahead regardless.

But I wanted you to be here.'

'Here for what?' John asked.

'You'll see, you'll see. What's that phrase you like? "All in good time".'

They strolled amiably, both in moccasins, down to the river's edge.

'Tell me what you've been up to, then, young man,' said the reverend.

'Well, Winnipeg gave me a taste of the white man's world. Regular food, soft beds, comforts I wasn't used to but grew to like. So I wanted to see what chance a boy from a tipi had of making a living in Calgary. Everyone talks about us indigenous people having to become good Canadian citizens and integrate with whites. I had to test out their hospitality.

'Chief Bearspaw agreed, so I made the journey, determined to succeed. I visited all the stores – no vacancies. I went to the railroad – no openings. Everywhere I looked, white men were being hired, but nobody wanted me, with or without an education. Then I was walking past the blacksmiths, and I heard a voice like yours, John – that lovely Scottish lilt. I wandered in and introduced myself.

' "The name's Maclean. George Maclean."

'This huge Scotsman roared with laughter, replying, "And I'm the Queen of Sheba. Now tell me who you really are."

'His name was Gregor MacLeod, and I told him about you and our story. He told me how the MacLeods and the Macleans had fought together against the Campbells. Perhaps he had a debt to repay. Either way, I could tell that he liked me, and he offered me a job on trial working with him for a dollar and a quarter a day. If I accepted, I could live in a tent at the back of the premises.

'I loved the work and the salty fellows I met. They taught me words I never knew existed. But when the harsh winter came the work dried up. No one else would hire me, so I had to go back to the reserve.

'I taught in the school for a while, but it wasn't for me. When a mounted police officer came onto the reserve and offered me a job as a police scout and guide, I jumped at the opportunity to go back to Calgary.

'In just a few months, the town had grown to nearly two thousand people. The place was changing on a daily basis. The Alberta Hotel had been built and was a sight to behold, with the longest bar in the Northwest Territories, not that I ever drank there. The town council had even taken the extreme step of prohibiting the firing of revolvers on the main street!

'I was once again in a soft bed, eating good food, and I was riding out with the Mounties chasing horse or cattle thieves, occasionally a murderer. At the end of the trail, wherever it was, I was expected to go in first with my rifle ready. Generally, there was no trouble, but I was always the one in greatest danger.

'They rewarded me for my bravery and complimented me on my work, but when I asked to join as a regular constable, I was politely turned down. I could be put to work by the police, undertake dangerous missions, be used as an aborigine to trap an aborigine, but I could not join the force. I was not surprised but disappointed, and I could not carry on working with them on that basis, so I returned to the reserve.

'Once at home, I tried to come to terms with everything. I know you care, and so do the McDougalls, but it is as plain as the antlers on a bull elk that most white men are utterly indifferent as to what happens to us. I had to decide what to do, return to Calgary to fashion a life where I would be more comfortable but neglected, or settle down on the reservation where I would lack material possessions but be part of the community.

'Then one day as I sat on a hill, Flora walked past. She is the daughter of Hector Crawler, who hunts grizzly bears and yet is still alive to tell the tale. He saw hard fighting, too, before being made a medicine man, and was known as brave, fearless and unbending as a pine stump.'

'Flora is a shy beauty with bright eyes and a modest temperament, and when I enquired about her skills, I was told she had inherited her mother's resourcefulness and her father's pride in his work. Apparently she makes the best moccasins in the Stoney camp, something I know you are qualified to talk about, John.

'She can sew robes from tipi covers, make good pemmican and moose lip soup, dishes from beaver, muskrat and porcupine meats, and when game is scarce, she can whip up tasty food from dandelion leaves, the inner bark of aspen trees and other edible plants.

'She stirs something in me, and when I look at her, she holds my gaze. That, in our society is the extent of courtship.'

George paused at John's raised eyebrow.

'And what happens if after the first months of marriage things do not work out?' John asked.

'Compatibility is tested, but generally after a couple of months, if things are good, separation is rare.'

John smiled at this.

'And when will the ceremony take place, George?'

'I have been waiting for you. Everything was primed for your arrival. I have agreed a price for Flora with Hector, but I wanted you here to witness our marriage.

Our marriages are quick, you know.

'Flora has made some moccasins for Wolf Ear, and then we will go to John McDougall's church to be blessed. Flora will come to my tipi at dark, and from then she will be with me till the day I die. You had until the next full moon, which is only a week away. I am glad that you have made it.'

John felt immense pride that George had put everything on hold, hoping his adoptive father would appear. The simplicity of Walking Buffalo's betrothal reminded Maclean of his own ascetic wedding. The reverend hoped that Walking Buffalo would be as happy with Flora as he was with Annie.

That evening, enjoying a pot of venison in Hector

Crawler's tipi, Walking Buffalo, his new bride, and the wedding party conversed in dialects, a tribute to the two missionaries' hard work mastering their language. All the time, Maclean wondered if this was to be his last official visit to the Stonies in a professional capacity. The reverend asked the young couple where they were going to set up their home, and everyone shifted uneasily where they sat.

George spoke, and the hush of his companions suggested he was representing the consensus of opinion in the tipi. 'You can tell many hours of talking have been spent on the subject, and still it is unresolved. Because of my own experience in Calgary, the decision is easy – we live on the reserve – but we must think of our children and grandchildren. Is it better to move now in the hope that conditions will improve in the future? Everyone has different views on the matter, and we cannot decide. I need time to think.'

After he waved Maclean off the following morning, Walking Buffalo went into the forest to be alone. It was like entering nature's cathedral, and he stayed there meditating past nightfall, waiting for a sign from the Great Spirit to suggest what he should do. It duly arrived in the form of rain, which doused a small prairie fire, stopping it in its tracks before it could take hold. George returned to Flora before sunrise, creeping into their tipi.

'I have the message from the Great Spirit that we have been waiting for. It is to stay here where we can do more for the Stonies, rather than living like a poor white man and woman in town.

'The land is not good for grain and would be better used for livestock. The vision I was given also included a permanent home made of wood. Our nomadic days are over, and we must abandon the tipi. We will have to lead by example, and I shall build us a home with the help of Hector before winter comes.'

Flora was overjoyed. Less used to the white man's ways, it was what she had wanted to hear. Chief Bearspaw called George to him when he heard the news.

'The decision for you not to go back to St John's College was the right one, and not to go to Calgary is also right. We Stonies need you more than the white community. I am making you a minor chief and a councillor, the youngest we have had in living memory. But your job is a big one: you must interpret the ways of the white man to us, and our ways to the white man. No easy task. You must do this with courage and honesty.'

John, meanwhile, had travelled home to tell Annie all about George and Flora's marriage, which she was thrilled about. They also talked further of their own future, though they knew the decision was out of their hands. The Blood mission would be discussed at the annual conference of the Methodist Church in Winnipeg in 1889. Only one of the board had visited the reserve, preferring to listen to the views of McDougall. It was he who effectively took the decision to close the mission, for a variety of reasons, but primarily for Maclean's failure to successfully convert anyone to the Methodist Church. It was a rationale Maclean would not and could not have argued with.

It was not a decision with immediate effect, and it would take almost another year for the Macleans to leave the missionary field. Whether or not Maclean would be replaced was as yet unclear. Three years earlier John had put forward plans that had been passed by the annual conference:

'There is much to learn in the training of men and women for missionary work. A few years of hard toil in these fields compels the worker, through ill health or other trying circumstances, to leave when, during that time, they have only been learning to toil.

'Who is to blame for this? Custom and a helpless conservatism that is wedded to an antiquated system... One year's training, under the guidance of a competent instructor, will prepare a young missionary to perform his work better than five years' self-education amongst these people.

'I can teach a young man to speak better and to understand the principles of the Blackfoot language more fully than I did after six years of hard study in the lodges with them as my teachers.

'A training course would save money by not being compelled to pay interpreters; besides the talents, time and energy expended would be employed so efficiently as to produce greater results.

'The matter of having aboriginal individuals as missionaries to their own people would make a marked difference too.'

It was never implemented.

In the time on the reserve remaining to him, the reverend was putting the finishing touches to his second book, *The Indians, Their Manners and Customs*, which was being published by the Methodist Book and Publishing House (and which, upon its release, in the autumn of 1889, received very good reviews).

He and Annie were also trying to finish their *Blackfoot Dictionary and Book of Grammar*, which had taken them most of their time on the reservation to compile. When the couple were finally advised of the decision to close the Blood mission, they were given further paid time to complete these works. However, they were crushed when they heard that Father JW Tims, another missionary, had just had his own *Blackfoot Grammar* published.

The reverend wrote a very complimentary letter to Father Tims, congratulating him on his achievement, although privately he felt the Anglican's book was not nearly as detailed as his and Annie's. Regardless, he knew finding a publisher for their work would now be nigh on impossible. He was right. To this day their handwritten work sits, unpublished, in the United Church Archives, Toronto.

As John travelled around the Blood reserve, he knew he was effectively saying goodbye, not only to his friends, but also to the land he had grown to love:

'Under the shadow of the grand old Rockies, breathing the air and freedom of the Western Prairies, I feel young again. Into the lodges, as in the days of yore, listening to the song and story of my dusky friends my heart is bounding with delight.

'I have been visiting the camps patiently telling people the strange tales of life among the white men. Gathering around me, the dwellers in the lodges have laughed and joked about the queer ways of the white people. Shaking my hand they then, one and all, said "Niokskatos is going to leave us, our hearts are on the ground!" Eagle-Arrow and Owl-Child came with sorrow depicted upon their countenances to tell me that all the people were very sorry.

'Calf-Shirt said, "I am going to come and see you at your home when you leave us.". The painted urchins in the lodges looked into my eyes laughing and shouted, "Niokskatos".

'Many of my old friends have gone to the Great Spirit during my service. Death has been busy among many lodges. The Blackfoot tongue, though, sounds sweeter to my ears than ever, and my heart yearns in pity for the helpless natives in their houses.

'Like innocent children they asked me whether or not I had seen any buffalo and when I answered "No" they appeared to feel keenly the import of what I said. "If only the buffalo would return again, we would feel happy," said one of the chiefs.

'Reverently they bowed their heads whilst in faith and humility we prayed. The shadows are falling over their pathway and they bow to the inevitable lot imposed upon them by the advent of the white race and the supremacy of their power.

'The redmen have the shadow and enjoy the sunshine of these latter days. The lodges are scattered along the river, sheltered from the winds by the fringes of timber, prairie fires are burning on every side of us and the mountains are wrapped in their snowy mantle, which they must soon lay aside when the gentle zephyrs from the west visit our prairie land.

'At evening time the ruddy glow of the prairie fires lights up the heavens and then their songs are heard as echoes of departing joys. In yonder camp up the river the medicine men are beating their drums and the patient sufferer awaits the time when the Great Spirit shall call him away.'

To ease his passage to a more likely posting at a growing town, the Missionary Society granted furlough to Maclean from December 1889 to March 1890. In this leave of absence, he was able to take Annie and their children home to Guelph for Christmas. It was a tumultuous home-coming, for it was five years since Annie had seen any of her family.

Meanwhile, the reverend had been invited to speak about his missionary experiences and native cultures at numerous venues, something he was only too glad to agree to. It was an eventful lecture tour, as he reflected later. 'In preparation for my own mission I had read as much as I could find out that was relevant. One such translated book was by the Frenchman Baron de Lahontan, who had actually lived amongst the Huron band and was influenced by a man named Adario who argued against "society" and sang the praises of natural religion, the fruits of which he saw as justice and a happy life.

'Adario looked with compassion on poor civilised man – a man without courage, without strength and someone incapable of providing himself with food and shelter. He never really lives because he is always torturing the life out of himself to clutch at wealth and honours which, even if he wins them, will prove to be but glittering illusions.

'For science and the arts are but the parents of corruption whereas the savage obeys the will of nature, his kindly mother. Therefore he is happy. It is civilised folk who are the real barbarians.

'I put forward Hobbes' philosophy that man's natural state was a state of war in which life was "solitary, poor, nasty, brutish and short", but said that I preferred the view of one of the founding fathers of the United States, Benjamin Franklin, who said,' "Savages we call them, because their manners differ from ours, which we think the perfection of civility; they think the same of theirs."

'Franklin praised their way of life, their customs, their councils, which reached agreement by discussions and consensus.

'He had respect for cultural diversity that was, and still is, ahead of its time. He had a fascination with nature and the natural origins of man and society. My audience listened intently for I could argue from a pragmatic standpoint.

'I supplemented my argument with reference to Jean-Jacques Rousseau, who put forward the case that civilisation with its envy and self-consciousness had made man bad and echoed what Adario had said. That the desire for reputation, honours and preferment devours us all in a rage to be distinguished, that we own what is best and worst in men – our virtues and our vices, our sciences and our errors, our conquerors and our philosophers – in short, a vast number of evil things and a small number of good.

'Rousseau praises indigenous people too, as they live a life that is simpler and more egalitarian than that of so called civilized man. Rousseau knows, however, we cannot go backwards to a primitive state but must act together in a properly constituted society that binds itself to its laws and reforms its systems of education.

'Not everybody agreed with my views but I was able to argue from a position of strength, having lived with aborigines, whom I characterised as a people who listened and could be persuaded by good argument. A people who have a high regard for their environment and look after it; who care for one another and have a sense of community that is at the core of their existence.

'I balanced this with my concerns and things I did not understand about their ways. Namely, their polygamous relationships and predilection for whiskey. But which societies do not have their problems?

'At the end of each lecture and now, towards the end of my tour of duty, I am beginning to feel a sense of worth return that Annie had tried to invoke in me and rekindle once again since my failure to convert them to Methodism.

'It has been a wholly justifiable leave of absence that has enabled me to reflect on the positive aspects of the mission. Prior to now I have felt a little anxious as to my future work but whenever I consider these doubts, I cast all my care upon God and I know that all will be well.

Chapter Thirteen

John spoke in many town halls and churches on his circuit of engagements, but one of the places he most liked the feel of was Moose Jaw. It was a fledgling town with a vibrant main street, and was expanding rapidly, so he was delighted when news reached him that this was to be his family's new base.

When he had been there, Maclean had enquired as to the history of the town and how it had come by its name. He was told that it came from a Cree expression, *Mocâstani-sîpiy*, meaning 'a warm place by the river', the first two syllables of which, when pronounced by the untutored tongue, sounded remarkably similar to Moose Jaw. There was also a local stretch of water that resembled the outline of a moose's jawbone. The combination of the two meant the name stuck.

During the peak years of the fur trade, Métis buffalo hunters wintered in cabins along the river valley, whilst the Cree and Assiniboine nations used the area as a winter encampment because it was well protected by the Coteau Range of hills. There was also a narrow river crossing at the confluence of the Moose Jaw River and

Thunder Creek, the latter given its name on account of the sudden storms that could blow up in the short, wet summers when warm and cold fronts converged on each other.

It was, however, the expansion of the Canadian Pacific Railway that led to its foundation as a recognised town. It was seen as an important railroad crossing, and the Canadian National Railway had a station there too. The abundance of water was seen as key to establishing service outposts for their steam locomotives, and a dam was built to ensure it would never run out.

The first work train arrived in September 1882, when Moose Jaw's business centre consisted of just five ragged tents, but by March 1883 there were six stores, five saloons, three hotels, two blacksmiths, one drugstore and forty houses. The first Methodist services were held in the waiting room of the CPR Depot, but by the end of the year a church had been built, quickly followed by another. The latter became known as 'The Little White Church', on account of its whitewashed clapperboard construction. It was where Maclean had spoken only months ago; now he was going back to this picturesque place of worship as its minister.

Before the reverend doctor departed the reserve for the last time, he went to Morley to see Walking Buffalo and tell him of his intended move. He found George and Flora in a log cabin beside a coulee on the south bank of the Bow River, due east of Morley. Together the couple had ridden over reservation trails, studying grass, trees and scenery, observing the birds and squirrels which lent such fascination to the countryside, before finally deciding on a plot still on the reservation but quite close to town.

The cabin was square, strong and attractive, mirroring its maker, and the couple had just had a baby girl whom they called Elizabeth. George had put up fences and was acquiring cattle and horses, with an aim to building fine herds. The couple were a picture of happiness and glad to show off the life they had created to the man who had been a distant but constant and positive influence on Walking Buffalo's life. Knowing that their meetings would be few and far between once John had moved to Moose Jaw, a distance of well over four hundred miles (680 kilometres), the two men agreed to write to each other regularly.

The Methodist Society had replaced Maclean with Mr Wells, who was a qualified teacher and regular church goer but not an ordained minister. The two had met briefly before John started out for Toronto, and the reverend admired what he saw. Wells was a man who, like Maclean a decade earlier, was full of optimism and keen to make a difference.

When John asked Mr Wells what his brief was, he received a clear and unequivocal reply: 'My job is to educate these people. Nothing more, nothing less. The mission is closed until such time as the society deems fit for it to be re-opened. I am to live in the house that you have built, and for that I thank you gladly. But can I ask you a question, doctor?'

Maclean nodded.

'I have asked for expenses to get me to my place of work, yet the society have only granted me three quarters of what I have asked, leaving me considerably out of pocket. Can you shed any light on that? Also, I know you and Annie have taught here, any advice?'

A wry smile was the best the reverend could offer, as he put his arm around the young teacher's shoulders.

'I wish I could be here to help you, for these are fine people. If you respect them they will pay you back double your investment. You must learn their language and get in tune with their spirituality. It is the key to their existence. Do not try to make things happen, for they cannot be coerced unless they believe what they are doing is right. They are not avaricious in any way, shape or form. In fact, they do not know the meaning of the word. They just want enough to survive on and be happy.

'If you can tap into their existential lifestyle, you will have succeeded. It is crucial that you do. Their education, your job, is the only way forward for them. If offers them a chance to integrate, to socialise and to achieve some sort of parity with the white man. Education is your guiding light. Ever should it be so. But as far as the remuneration is concerned, forget it. The society sees teachers and missionaries as vocational emissaries, and the sooner you realise that, the sooner you will come to terms with your lot. Good luck, my friend!'

Wells thanked Maclean for his words of wisdom, and the reverend set off for Toronto, anxious to be present for the arrival of his fifth child, due in early September. The existence of the Canadian Pacific Railway had eased matters of removal hugely, and Maclean's large library of books, which first of all had to go to Guelph, was shipped without concern. Items were simply boxed, paid for and transported.

As the reverend travelled back, he realised how

much things had changed. No rivers to swim his horses across, no wagons to pull, no hostile indigenous bands to avoid, no buffalo to hold them up, no lack of water to drink, no bull flies to swat... Things were immeasurably easier, but were they any better? John reflected on the passage of a decade as he rode the rails home, but ever the optimist, he preferred to look forward rather than back.

He'd estimated the route from Moose Jaw to Toronto to be about 1700 miles (2735 km). He arrived back in Guelph in the middle of August, desperate to see his family again, and found himself enveloped by Richie, Walter, Owie and Peggy-Sue (although John remained defiant in the face of insubordination and continued to call his only daughter 'Alice').

As he wrapped his children in his arms, John realised how much they had grown in his absence. They were all trying to talk to him at the same time, and he could not make head nor tail of what they were saying, apart from the words 'Dotty! Dotty! Dotty!' It was then that Annie appeared on the veranda of the Barker's home. She was a picture of loveliness and smiled at her husband in such a giving way, yet her eyes were glassy and filled with tears. She held a babe in her arms.

Their child had come early. He ran to his wife and wrapped his arms around her, anxious to repay all the support she had afforded him over the previous decade. 'Meet Dorothy,' Annie said to her husband.

'Dorothy?' asked a quizzical John, not entirely sure of the name.

'You and I are ageing but so far as I'm aware, your hearing is intact, John. This is Dorothy.'

John smiled, in his enigmatic way conceding to his wife's choice of name.

'Hello, my darling Dorothy. Pleased to meet you, I'm sure.'

Annie explained that 'Dotty', as her brethren called her, had arrived three or four weeks early but was as healthy as could be. The only worry was the accuracy of her name: she really was like a 'dot', and very small even given her premature arrival.

Annie was upset that their second daughter's arrival had not been witnessed by John, and felt she was responsible for this.

John put her mind at rest. He was just so glad to be back in the bosom of his family. No blame should be apportioned, no blame assumed. They should be thankful for what they had, and that was the end of the matter.

There followed a busy couple of weeks as they prepared to set off for Moose Jaw. There was much for John to consider: a new decade, a new job and a new addition to the family.

As they travelled up to their Saskatchewan destination by train, John commented to Annie how nice it would be not to have to build the house they would live in. Their children were remarkably well behaved on the journey, for it was as much an adventure for them as it was for their parents. With so many young ones to entertain her, Dotty was perfectly happy the whole journey, too.

They were met in their new town by James Hamilton Ross and Stewart Battle, both prominent members of the community, who had been amongst the first settlers in Moose Jaw. They had been present at the inaugural CPR Waiting Room Methodist Service and had heard John speak on his tour seven years later. When a vacancy opened in their church, they had made overtures to the Methodist Society to get the charismatic preacher appointed to them.

The contrast between his arrivals in Fort Macleod and Moose Jaw could not have been more marked, and it was not lost on Maclean. At Fort Macleod, at first he had been treated with suspicion, kept at a distance by both whites and indigenous bands. In Moose Jaw, he was welcomed with open arms, lauded even.

J.H. Ross was a highly motivated character. In 1884, he had been instrumental in setting up a provisional Board of Education, which he also chaired, for the public education of the children of the burgeoning town. After this, he had decided to run for mayor, and his nomination speech outlined his priorities:

'As for the need of a school, let me say that education is one of the most sacred responsibilities entrusted to parents.

'Education is a matter for the home, and when more formal instruction is required, it should be a matter of choice. Many citizens are willing to share that responsibility with the church but not with government.'

He was elected, and there followed a number of temporary school buildings including a makeshift leanto classroom in the Moose Hotel, before an eight-room school house was built and opened in 1890.

Ross wanted to involve Maclean not only in formal worship within the school but also as someone who could initiate debates with the older pupils, having seen him previously co-ordinate question and answer sessions. The reverend doctor would be helping to establish the school as a permanent institution in Moose Jaw, and also beginning the formal education of his own children, with Richie and Walter to attend school for the first time.

The two Maclean brothers were slightly anxious about the formalities expected of them at school. Aboriginal life revolved around a lack of structure. They slept when they were tired and ate when they were hungry (and food was available). The concept of time was irrelevant. You did what you did when you wanted to do it. Theirs had been a spontaneous existence, although Annie and John had always tried to balance it with a much more rigorous lifestyle in their own home.

Ross was an enlightened individual, and he was keen to facilitate this integration of cultures. He had read Maclean's recent book, *The Indians, Their Manners and Customs*, and agreed with many of its assertions. Trying to change people of their own generation's opinion was hard because people were set in their ways. The best chance was to educate them whilst young.

In his book, Maclean attacked certain stereotypes of the indigenous people held by the whites, such as the notion 'that the Indian is naturally lazy'.

What the reverend doctor had seen first-hand was how 'the white man had introduced different kinds of work to that which the red man is accustomed to attend to. The red man has not been trained to do these jobs and hence that particular toil is not congenial to him.

'Conversely, the white man will soon tire if he attempts to follow the hunting habits of the Indian.'

Maclean called for a 'just appreciation of the work that belonged to every individual whatever race, colour or creed they belonged to'.

He believed that the church and the state needed to work in 'a necessary partnership. Training the Indian, as true civilisation should do, includes the work of both these agencies.

'It should not be antagonistic. The one should complement the other, resulting in unity of labour, not one taking precedence over the other'.

Maclean always reflected on what he could have done better in his own work, feeling the only way to improve was to accept criticism positively and learn from things that had not gone well. He sensed a lack of openness from the church and state that was hindering progress.

He called for 'a certain level of mutual criticism between the church and the state that would promote helpfulness as long as each did not overstep its bounds'.

Maclean was a staunch supporter of the aboriginals' rights to their land, granted by treaty in a time when, particularly in the United States, they were under tremendous pressure to give up their lands for white settlement. And quite apart from their rights, he pointed out that the presence of aboriginal people meant the creation of commercial opportunities and jobs to supply them. In any case, 'there must be equal rights for all, rights that must be sacredly revered and upheld'. J.H. Ross could not have agreed more.

One of Maclean's favourite contentions was that 'the criticism of work being done with the Indians arises from ignorance about the Indians and too much is being expected too soon'.

He felt that a number of government agencies were being too heavy handed: 'Direct opposition to native customs will stir up strife and the object sought will be lost; but if the religious, social, political and domestic customs are thoroughly understood and discretion used on imparting others, there will result abundant success'.

Maclean suggested that the two cultures were both on the road to civilisation, albeit at different rates, but 'that the culture of one should be studied and admired as honestly as the other'.

As somebody who had lived amongst the indigenous people and learnt their language, Maclean was in an ideal position to translate their ideas, concepts and stories in the manner and spirit in which they were intended.

His attention to detail in studying the native customs and language came at the beginning of the modern study of ethnology, and Maclean's observations were valued by pioneers in the field such as Dawson, Boas, Pilling and Lowie.

Open and healthy discussions about all these issues were seen by the Board of Education as crucial for the development of an equitable society; the culture fostered in school would, in time, filter into the mainstream culture, creating the type of town they all wanted to live in.

Thanksgiving and Christmas came upon the Macleans in a trice. They had been in Moose Jaw just over three months and were already firmly settled. The plan was to enjoy the festive season at home, because of all of

John's church commitments, and then travel down to Guelph to see in the New Year.

Over Christmas the weather took a turn for the worse, with cold winds blowing across the valley and right through the town. Dorothy picked up a chill, and while the family tried not to worry about her, she was still very small, and travel arrangements were put on hold.

Some hastily made rearrangements resulted in Stewart Battle and his family inviting John round to their house on New Year's Eve. His son, Henry, was Richie's best friend. Annie was going to stay at home and look after Dotty.

Mr and Mrs Battle turned their living room into a dormitory to house the Maclean children as well as their three young ones. Cushions, eiderdowns and blankets adorned every bit of soft furnishing as they tried to entertain and then placate their young guests. John slipped out to check on his wife and was distressed to find Dorothy with a raging temperature. She had developed a worrying fever.

They flannelled her down. She was burning up on the coldest of nights. It wasn't long before she had a febrile fit and they thought they'd lost her. They hadn't then, but an hour later, in the early hours of New Year's Day, Dorothy, not strong enough to cope with her fever, perished in the arms of her mother and father.

John had seen dead children in the course of his work. In fact, dealing with infant mortality had become an everyday occurrence, a galling necessity of missionary life. He had never forgotten burying Siochki, his friend's son. Now he knew he would be doing the same for his own daughter.

As a lad who had travelled from the poor areas of Glasgow, born of a father and grandfather both tainted by alcoholism, the Reverend Doctor John Maclean had come a long way. This event, however, shook him to the core, because it was a life lost before it had really started. He wanted to give up his soul and sacrifice it so that Dotty could live, but he knew the world didn't work like that.

It took months and months to come to terms with the loss of their daughter, but the Macleans kept busy and at the height of summer were cheered when one Saturday lunchtime Annie told the family that she was expecting their sixth child, who was due to join them close to Christmas.

After they had eaten, John took Richie around to Henry Battle's house for a sleepover. The reverend stayed for a cup of tea with the family. He got on well with Stewart, who was a town councillor and school governor and had a keen intellect. They would talk about all manner of things, but the one topic John dared not mention was fishing. Stewart was a fanatical angler and had infected his eldest, Henry, and Richie with the same bug.

John could not understand the attraction. He was a useless fisherman himself, having wasted many hours on the Blood reserve trying to catch his supper, all to no avail. As soon as Stewart started to talk about a new reel that he'd bought for his rod, Maclean playfully jumped up, citing it as his cue to return home.

Stewart invited the reverend to join him, Henry and Richie on their fishing expedition to Thunder Creek the following afternoon. Maclean turned him down, joshingly explaining that 'never in a month of Sundays will I voluntarily fish. It would be under penance and that, hopefully, will never happen.'

Stewart laughed and wished the reverend doctor good evening, adding that he was looking forward to John's sermon in church the following morning. Once at home, Maclean read through his notes for Sunday, made a few amendments, then joined Annie on the veranda of their modest house.

Annie said that the children were difficult to settle because of the unusually warm and blustery conditions. It felt like it was going to storm but the weather couldn't make up its mind as they sat on the porch bench swinging gently to and fro. They retired to bed slightly earlier than normal.

Almost as soon as John's head was on the pillow, he was fast asleep. But he was awoken by a dream in the middle of the night. In it, someone was rattling the front door and banging continuously with their fist. Only it wasn't a dream. As John sat up, he sensed an orange glow from the open window as the curtains danced in the strong breeze.

He stuck his head out of the window to find Stewart Battle below. John couldn't see flames, but he'd seen enough prairie fires to know something was ablaze.

'We're fine on this side of town, John,' his friend told him, 'but on the far side a fire has taken hold. I came to get you. The fire department need all possible help. I suggest we leave our families asleep. If we wake them they'll only get scared, and we'll have time to come and move them if necessary.'

John relayed all this to Annie, who agreed with the plan of action. She got up and packed some bags just in case they needed to evacuate. She knew how quickly fire could spread, especially on such a windy night. She watched from an upstairs window, ready to stir the children at the first sign of approaching flames.

John and Stewart ran towards the centre of town to see what help they could offer. The fire was raging in the business district, and there were lots of people helping to douse the flames.

Eight years earlier, in 1883, when the town was still establishing itself, a fire had broken out in a store on River Street West. In response, a fire department had been created and five years later a fire station built, with one small fire engine. As in the early days the town's construction had been primarily of timber, the council had taken the precaution of installing large water tanks at strategic points over the town.

They played a crucial part in managing to contain the fire so that within a couple of hours the flames were under control. The fire chief thanked everyone for coming to help and released the majority of the public in the early hours of the morning. His crew and a reserve brigade had everything under control.

John and Stewart returned home to their anxious wives. Their children had slept blissfully through everything. Things could have been worse had the fire started in the residential part of town, where casualties would have been much higher than the three dead the fire claimed.

Twenty-six buildings were lost, including the older church, and of the forty-one businesses operating in

Moose Jaw, all of them were severely affected. John's clapperboard church was thankfully untouched, and early that morning he went to open up, not to preach, but to let people meet and pray if they wished. By midday most people had talked or prayed themselves out and returned home. John was thankful for the respite.

He got home to find Annie had invited the Battles to lunch. In times of need, the community was good at pulling together, and although the children were unaware of the seriousness of the situation, the parents needed company to air their emotions.

Talking things through helped the adults, whilst the children remained gloriously oblivious to the implications of all that had happened. Henry and Richie pestered Stewart about their fishing trip, and he conceded he still wanted to go. It was only a short walk up to Thunder Creek, and a couple of hours angling would help take his mind off proceedings. The boys couldn't find a good reason why fishing should be cancelled, apart from the weather, which continued to swirl in irregular hot and cold blasts of air.

Henry's siblings were two younger sisters, and Richie was like the brother he had always wanted. All agreed it would be an enjoyable afternoon for the three of them. Walter and Owie protested at their exclusion, but John was adamant that the pair needed to demonstrate patience and perseverance before being allowed to go fishing.

Once up at Thunder Creek, Stewart felt the weight of events from the previous evening slip from his shoulders, and the three of them cast their lines. Nothing seemed to be biting, so Stewart got out his knife to cut down two 'Y' shape branches. He impaled them in the ground and rested Henry and Richie's rods on the supports, enabling them to go and climb trees whilst it was quiet.

Stewart loved the solitude of the creek. It was one of his favourite places, but in all the years he had fished there, he had only ever enjoyed modest success in what he'd caught. It never bothered him though; he saw it as a pastime rather than a sport.

The boys returned from their tree climb to drink some lemonade Annie had put in a rucksack, as Stewart bemoaned the fact he had not had a single bite for over an hour. Richie looked at him as though the solution was obvious.

'What's that look for, young Maclean?' asked Stewart of his charge.

'Well, sir, you're using a float to fish. It's going to storm, so the fish are staying deeper in the water. If you don't mind me saying so, Mr Battle, you need to put a weight on your line. Then you might have a chance of catching one.'

Richie was a model of politeness and respect, and Stewart was not in the least bit offended by his opinions; however he did disagree with Richie's weather prediction.

'It's not going to storm. It's been threatening to for a couple of days now, and nothing has materialised. How we'd have loved some rain last night though. That would have helped.'

Nevertheless, Stewart adjusted his line.

'The fish will be in the middle of the creek,' said Richie. 'It may be faster flowing, but they're safer there.

That's where you need to cast.'

Stewart was intrigued by this young man's confidence.

'How do you know all this, Richie?'

'Eagle-Arrow and Owl-Child taught me,' he replied, matter-of-factly. 'Look at those clouds, Mr Battle. They're as tall as they are wide. That's a sure sign of storm. The swifts that were cutting circles in the sky have gone...'

Stewart looked up and nodded.

'And the squirrels that were collecting nuts and berries have disappeared. Listen...' It was eerily quiet.

'Wildlife will always tell you what's happening. A storm will hit soon.'

At that moment Stewart's line went taut. He'd never felt a fish this heavy. The excitement surged through every sinew. He felt electrified by his potential catch. His new reel seemed to be worth every dollar at this precise moment. If only his line would hold.

His switchblade sat in his pocket, and he was prepared to cut the line if it threatened his new purchase. He tried to estimate the fish's weight as it fought, but it was a useless diversion. He needed all his energy to try and land this fish.

Richie had been caught in storms before. He didn't mind getting wet. But this wasn't the open prairie, this was so called Thunder Creek. As Mr Battle fought with his catch, Richie looked up at the clouds. The bright rays that had filtered through earlier had now been obliterated by a threatening gloom. Everywhere was dark. A swirling vortex of grey seemed to be sucking the life out of the area.

'I'm going to commend you to your father for such sound advice about my line,' Stewart shouted out to him. 'I can't believe I'm going to land a fish of this size. Boys, bring the landing net over here.'

They obliged. They could now see the thrashing specimen close to the surface.

'Don't worry, gents. If you sense lightning, count the seconds before you hear the thunder. Each second counts as approximately one mile, so we'll have time to get to the crag – *if* it comes, that is.'

'Unless...' said Richie,

'Unless what?' replied the preoccupied angler.

'Unless the first strike is directly overhea—'

CRAACCK!

Silence.

In town the rain thudded into the remnants of the twenty-six buildings destroyed by fire, hissing like the devil was exhaling. Had it come but twenty-four hours earlier, perhaps things might have been different.

The electrical storm had been followed almost immediately by an intense downpour. Flash floods created small rivers of water trying to find an escape route down drains, which were soon overflowing. For half an hour a thunderous sound echoed from above, from below and from all angles, before it subsided, the cold front pushing its warmer cousin out of the way.

The air felt clean and fresh in the Maclean household as John mopped up a leak in the kitchen. Annie was entertaining Walter, Owie and Alice in the lounge. The children loved her animated and dramatic readings. She spoke about the Bible being the most wonderful book, full of poetry, history, mythology and amazing stories, and when she picked it up, it signified fun to the children.

She didn't so much as read from the Bible as use it as a reference point. When the storm had started, she'd flicked to Genesis 6-9, the story of Noah's Ark, and sent the children scurrying to their rooms to collect their toys, many of them small carvings of animals made by the women on the Blood reserve.

On a tray they made a procession leading to a wooden fruit bowl that doubled as the Ark. Once John had finished mopping up, they then decamped to the kitchen and slowly filled the sink with water – the flood was coming.

John watched his wife closely. She was totally engaged in what she was doing. With various chairs and stools supporting their different heights, Walter, Owie and Alice splashed in the deluge, rescuing animals that had fallen overboard. As the floorboards took another soaking, John wondered why he had bothered to clear up at all. But it mattered not.

Annie pulled the plug to signify the rains were subsiding and the waters receding. They used towels to wipe and dry the figures as calm descended on the world. Annie explained how the story of the flood paralleled the story of creation.

The world was in fact a cycle of creation, un-creation and re-creation, in which the ark played a pivotal role. From the simplest of re-enactments came a clear message about life. John could not help himself and applauded instinctively. He had been transported, just as their children had, to another world, another time. His heart was filled with joy at what he'd just witnessed.

Annie asked John to go and get Richie from the Battle's house. She was sure they'd have come back before the storm. John deferred the request, saying how much Richie and Henry enjoyed each other's company. He'd go in an hour or so; in the meantime they would get the children ready for bed. Although it was only early evening, they were 'an early to bed, early to rise' family. Once the children were all clean, with their faces scrubbed, and wrapped in the dressing gowns that Annie had made, the three children sat in the lounge waiting for a cup of warmed milk. They loved the feeling of homeliness and warmth as their bellies were filled. Annie always insisted that children were creatures of comfort and routine, and as far as her children were concerned, she was right.

'Where is Richie?' asked Owie, who idolised his brother.

'Your father has gone to collect him from Henry's house. Don't worry, Owie, he'll be home soon.'

John walked up the path to Stewart's house and knocked on the door. Mary, his wife, was upstairs but shouted to whoever it was to 'come in'. The reverend stood in the hallway after closing the front door behind him.

'Mary. It's me, John. What's Stewart doing with the boys?' There was no immediate response, just the sound of footsteps. Mary appeared at the top of the stairs,

'I'm just sorting the girls out for bedtime, John. I felt sure they were with you.'

The reverend doctor's heart skipped a beat as he pondered what to do next. Mary looked with concern at a man she trusted implicitly.

'I suspect they took refuge under the crag and have gone back for some evening fishing.' The crag was an overhanging piece of rock close to Thunder Creek that offered protection from the elements.

'I'll go and fetch them, Mary. The scoundrels, staying out so late. I hope they've got a good catch.' John tried to make light of matters, but both he and Mary were palpably on edge.

John started off towards Thunder Creek, and a horse and wagon overtook him, going in the same direction. Sunday evening was normally a relatively quiet time in Moose Jaw, but the reverend was disquieted by a sense of activity. His heart rate quickened again. In the distance he saw a dark figure walking towards him. Was that Stewart? No, but he recognised the gait.

As he got closer, the approaching man slowed his walk to a funereal pace. It was James Hamilton Ross, the mayor. His countenance told John everything. The mayor could not speak. He simply shook his head and turned his body to allow John to pass.

As fast as a forty-year-old's legs could carry him, John ran. When he got to the creek he saw three shrouded bodies being laid on the wagon. If he didn't know it before, he knew it now. His eldest son, his eldest son's best friend and his own friend were dead.

John got to the wagon in a breathless state, where Doc' Watson stood with a couple of other men. John's desperate look begged an explanation.

'It was lightning, John... would have been mercifully quick... three cardiac arrests... they were probably standing close together... even if they weren't, the strike will have forked. These two gentlemen came up here to fish after the storm and ran back to get me and Ross... there was nothing...'

The doc's staccato speech tailed off. He intimated which body was Richie's, and John unfurled the sodden torso to take one last look at the boy who had given him such immense pride. John laid his head on his son's chest and wept and wept.

The three men standing close by walked to the edge of the creek to allow John to grieve. When he could cry no more, he wrapped his son's body back up in the shroud and gathered himself.

The grief he felt was immeasurable, but his sense of duty told him he had to go and tell Annie and their children and then see Mary, who not only had lost her son but her husband too. But first John wanted to go to his church and lay the bodies to rest there overnight.

Once they had done so, John brushed down his clothes and spent some moments in private prayer.

He asked the Lord for strength to carry out his immediate task of telling both families such terrible news, and for continued guidance to follow the right path. He realised as he spoke that Annie's parable of Noah's Ark and the cycle of creation had probably been given just after the three had perished. In a strange sort of way, the notion comforted him.

John dwelt upon that thought as he walked towards his home, where his pregnant wife waited. It was the longest walk of his life.

Chapter Fourteen

The family looked to each other for support, as well as accepting offers of help from their tight knit community. Later in the year, the arrival of Albert, who quickly became Bertie, accelerated the healing process somewhat. John's work was changing too. Freedom from his missionary responsibilities enabled the reverend doctor to further cultivate his parallel career as a historian and author, which he'd started on the Blood reserve.

His next book followed up on the work he had done learning the Blackfoot language. *James Evans, the Inventor of the Cree Syllabic*, a biography, was published in Toronto. The book characterised John's keen interest in indigenous culture, ethnology and people.

He always had a project on the go. When one book was finished, he simply started another. However, a book might take him a couple of years to put together, so he kept up with contemporary issues via pamphlets, religious tracts, articles, serials and numerous short stories, all of which were published in a wide variety of secular periodicals.

As a keen man of letters, Maclean maintained an extensive correspondence with ethnologists such as Horatio Hale, J.C. Pilling and Franz Boas. The latter, who worked at Harvard University, was in charge of a conference, the World Exposition of Ethnology and Archaeology, which was to be held in Chicago.

Boas wrote to Maclean asking him to collect a selection of physical measurements of the Blackfoot population, as well as artefacts for the exposition. He gave John the official title of 'Observer for the Canadian North-West' for this role.

It gave the reverend doctor an excuse to make a trip back to the Blood reserve. It was a distance of some five hundred miles, which in the past would have been a major undertaking, but all he had to do now was jump on a train to Calgary. Along the way, John recorded his thoughts in his journal:

'If ever a railway has been instrumental in embracing the concept of an overarching nationhood, it is the Canadian Pacific Railway. It has knitted all its disparate parts together to help define the nation of Canada and give it an identity.'

Walking Buffalo was only a short distance from Calgary, and Maclean could stop off there en route to the Blood reserve. The reverend wrote to George to ask if it was all right to stay for a few days in a month or so's time. Once more, trains aided much quicker lines of communication.

When the reverend doctor greeted his adopted son on his ranch, he found him the proud owner of a farm predominantly of cattle, but with some horses, sheep, chicken, ducks and geese too. John was hugely impressed. He was invited in to meet Tatanga Mani's growing family and wanted to know everything. How had George decided on stock? How had he set things up? What problems had he encountered? Over the next few days, the two talked long into the night.

George explained that, initially, he had had to decide between keeping horses or cattle. He had decided on the latter because his peers were reluctant to think of horses as farm animals. Horses had been adopted as aids for warfare and hunting, and were amongst a man's proudest possessions. Not only that, but horse stealing was their greatest outdoor pastime.

Cattle could be stolen, of course, but they could not be driven at a highwayman's gallop from one camp to another, nor could cattle contribute much to the conducting of inter-tribal rivalry.

Missionaries preached that horse stealing was wrong, whilst the Mounted Police outlawed it. Indigenous peoples, however, remained unconvinced, and horses continued to move back and forth between the Blood and Stoney reservations much more extensively than authorities realised.

Horse stealing was seen as a game of skill with horses as the stake. George explained that a Stoney called John Rocky Mountain had an especially fine pinto that, for years, had periodically changed hands because it was beautifully marked and so fleet of hoof. Within a week he would always recover it, and preferably a few extra ones, taking them back to the Bow River.

George was tempted to keep horses; he knew more about them than cattle. Boys raced their horses and never hesitated to test their skills on a bronco, a mustang or a known bucker. They commonly rode bareback with a pair of rawhide laces passing through the horse's lower jaw acting as the bridle. They learned to hang entirely on one side of a galloping mount, to use the animal's body as a shield against enemy arrows or bullets. But despite all his equine knowledge, George felt keeping cattle was a safer bet.

He started with a small herd, which he built up until one devastating winter wiped out over half his stock. Many cattlemen were forced out of business, and some older Bloods said it was the Great Spirit's way of voicing his displeasure about raising cattle inside barbed wire fences. Walking Buffalo made it clear to others on the reservation that he was not going to abandon cattle raising because of a single setback.

He said he would build his herd back up to its former size, and that is what he did. In due course, George became the leading producer of livestock on the reservation, proving beyond all doubt that ranching could succeed on their lands.

George's livelihood was secure, he was a minor chief: his life was a demonstration to his fellow Bloods as to how with the right approach they could thrive in their changing world. He felt vindicated in his decision to stay on the reservation, and this loyalty was rewarded by his father-in-law, Hector Crawler, who nominated George to succeed him as medicine man. Hector was getting on in years and recognised it was time to step down from his role as the highest tribal authority on medical, spiritual and moral matters.

The Bloods believed that for all human disorders there were specific remedies that the Great Spirit had thoughtfully placed in the great range of native plants. The medicine man had to study the curative properties of herbs and roots and zealously guard the secrets of his high calling until he had trained his successor. Hector chose his son-in-law because George was largely self-educated about plants and herbal remedies and possessed such good sense.

Old Hector was a good teacher. He knew about tracking grizzly bears, about forecasting weather, about communing with the Great Spirit and about preparing medicine. He took Walking Buffalo into the hills and forests to show him how to acquire the requisite spiritual understanding to become a good medicine man.

Hector explained the secrets of the animals, such as why the otter perpetually wore an amused smile on his face and why the wolverine had an angry frown. Long ago, the forest creatures had wanted to teach the wolverine a lesson, as he was behaving in a selfish and unfriendly way.

Otter, acting as spokesperson for everyone, approached the wolverine with a problem that needed sorting. She said, 'Skunk is being a real nuisance, wolverine, leaving unpleasant smells everywhere. We have all agreed that someone must plug skunk's scent ducts with spruce gum and put an end to the odours that he pollutes the lovely evenings with. But nobody has stepped forward to fulfil this dangerous task. That is why I am here to ask you, the bravest of the brave. What do you say?'

Flattered by otter's compliments, wolverine accepted the challenge. But startling skunk as he crept up on him, he got a full dose of the animal's smelly defence right in his face. The otter has been grinning ever since, and the wolverine has never lost the smell, hence his bitter and vengeful demeanour. Folklore tales such as this were seen as important to pass on as technical tips.

Hector showed George how the liquid from boiled Saskatoon bark possessed healing qualities when applied to wounds, how a brew made from the buds of black poplar would relieve throat and chest disorders, and how seneca root would help all manner of ailments. They gathered supplies of chokecherry bark, balsam buds, yarrow leaves and dandelion shoots so Walking Buffalo could keep a store of them to be used in winter.

Hector taught George the medicine man's songs and dances and helped him choose some suitable headwear for his exalted position. The custom of adorning headpieces with horns was very old, but the buffalo horns George chose not only echoed his name but symbolised strength and honour, as the buffalo was considered to be a very special gift from the Great Spirit.

He didn't know it yet, but in the course of time, Walking Buffalo's horns were to earn him fame, not only in his community but in the Calgary Stampede and finally in the many countries of the world he would visit.

In the morning George gave the reverend doctor some moccasins, a mirror case with a beaded neck strap, a smoking pipe and some bags for holding face paints, all to be sent to Chicago for the World Exposition of Ethnology. More items were collected from the Blood reserve, which was another enlightening visit.

Although much quicker, the journey home was as reflective on a train as it was on horseback, and it enabled John to take stock of things. It was a different experience viewing the Blood reserve as a visitor rather than an occupant. He was able to look more dispassionately at the situation and realised, despite his inability to find Methodist converts, that overall his and Annie's contribution was something he was proud of.

John was forty years of age and had been in Canada for nearly twenty years. An ordained minister with a decade's missionary experience under his belt, he had three books published, three degrees attained and a family that was once again burgeoning. All this rolled around in his head as John covered the tracks back to Moose Jaw. Eventually, worn out by his thoughts, he slept.

When he woke it was from a dream that had taken him back to Glasgow. It was the first time since emigrating that he had felt the draw to go back home to Scotland.

That evening John relayed the story to Annie, who looked into her husband's eyes. She could see this man who had so enchanted her with his foreignness needed to visit his homeland, and yet she knew taking Bertie and the others was not viable.

Annie co-ordinated the Lecture Tour with the aim of raising funds for a new church in Moose Jaw and invited Eagle-Arrow and Owl-Child to accompany John. There was an emotional reunion when the reverend presented each brother with a pair of moccasins he had made during the transatlantic crossing.

Hamish reflected joshingly, ' 'Tis twenty years since we've seen you, brother. You've done well for yourself. Never mind a man with letters after his name, but a man who writes letters into the bargain – a guiding light, you might say.

'You were always a man with values, a man who knew what he wanted and went out to get it. And here you stand today, a man with good taste, a man who has seen more of the world than we could ever dream of seeing, and what do you bring us from halfway around the world? A pair of slippers each!'

All apart from John, Eagle-Arrow and Owl-Child roared with laughter. Within seconds the brothers composed themselves, realising a faux-pas of some sort.

'Why the stony faces, John?' Hamish enquired.

This time John did laugh.

'You compound your gaffes, my brothers,' he said. 'The Stonies are the Blood's tribal rivals. It's like accusing a Maclean of being a Campbell. And the moccasin is of huge cultural and spiritual importance to them, a bit like the kilt to a Scotsman. To laugh at them is disrespectful.'

The brothers cringed at their social ineptitude, and made their apologies to Eagle-Arrow and Owl-Child, who accepted them with the good grace with which they were offered.

Arriving back in Moose Jaw with a sizeable amount of capital enabled work on a new Methodist Church to be started almost straight away. Before the end of that year, 1892, Maclean saw another book published, on the life of one of the pioneer missionaries, Henry B. Steinhauer, the building work of the church completed and news of a new posting to Port Arthur, Ontario.

Life was never dull with the reverend doctor.

Chapter Fifteen

It was the Methodist way to move pastors on every three to four years, presenting them with fresh challenges. After the new church was built, the reverend doctor would have liked some more time in Moose Jaw to enjoy the fruits of his labours, but it wasn't to be. He packed his family up to travel the 830 miles (1,350 km) or so to the edge of Lake Superior.

Port Arthur had also prospered from the CPR construction boom, but after the completion of the railway line, the company had moved its operations to the lower Kaministiquia River, abruptly reducing business in the port. Not only that, but silver mining, which had been a mainstay of the local economy since the 1870s, had ended in 1890, when the US Congress had cut off the profitable trade into their country.

Maclean found his new posting to be a depressed town in need of spiritual support, and he threw himself into his job with customary vigour. He was given extra responsibilities by his church when he was made secretary and then president of the Manitoba and North West Conferences, which honoured the contribution he had made to their organisation.

The reverend doctor continued to write and had two more books published whilst in Port Arthur. A daughter, Evelyn, was born, and Alice was thrilled to have another sister. In 1896, they were soon on their way again, this time heading for the more picturesque town of Neepawa, within the province of Manitoba.

It was a place similar to Moose Jaw, the town's name coming from a Cree word meaning 'Land of Plenty'. The family loved it there. The rolling hills around the town were fabulous places to play, and the area to the north had forests to explore, and for the children to use the skills that Eagle-Arrow and Owl-Child had imparted.

It was where the family welcomed its last member, in 1899, when Willard was born. In deference to Britain's Liberal ex-prime minister, who had died the year before, his middle name was given as Gladstone.

While the reverend doctor enjoyed discussing national politics, he had been scarred by the interdenominational rivalry between himself and Samuel Trivett while on the Blood reserve. He was dismayed when the conflict reared its head again, as soon as he set foot in Neepawa. This time, however, the political turmoil between the two churches had national implications, ultimately leading to the downfall of the government.

For many years, the province of Manitoba had publicly funded separate schools for Catholics and Protestants, French being spoken in the Catholic schools and English in the Protestant ones. But when the provincial government withdrew public funding for Catholic education, there was uproar. The national

Conservative government, who supported this action, were defeated at the next election, and the new Liberal government advocated tolerance. Nevertheless, by the end of the century, French was no longer supported as an official language in Manitoba, which led to a strengthening of French-Canadian nationalism in Quebec.

When previously the reverend doctor had discussed church politics with Walking Buffalo, his adopted son shook his head and said, 'The Great Spirit has no denominations. He welcomes everyone. Why hasn't the white man shown more of the tolerant understanding he talks about? Remember, the Indian has a perfect right to be an Indian; he need never be ashamed of it. You are not one of the white men who try and make us be like white men, but there are many of you who try and force their culture upon us.

'If white people want to help the Indian, they should take your example and get to know him better. They would understand why he wants to keep his Indian ways. Indians know the meaning of brotherhood under one Great Spirit, or God, as you call him.

'We Indians have always recognised a kinship between ourselves and all other living things. Animals, birds, insects, flowers and trees, all of us are children of one Great Spirit. And nobody tries to make the coyotes act like beavers or the eagles behave like robins.

'Do you know that trees talk? Well, they do. They talk to each other, and they'll talk to you if you listen. Trouble is, white people don't listen. They never listen to the Indian, and I don't suppose they'll listen to the other voices in nature. But I have learned a lot from trees, sometimes about the weather, sometimes about animals, sometimes about the Great Spirit.

'Civilised people depend too much on man-made printed pages. I turn to the Great Spirit's book, which is the whole of his creation. You can read a big part of that book if you study nature. I have studied in nature's university – the forests, the rivers, the mountains and the animals, which includes us. Shall I broaden the debate?

'Long ago my people fought with bows and arrows, and only a few warriors were killed. Nowadays, warring nations are not satisfied with killing a few; they aim to destroy thousands – and in the future it will be millions, mark my words.

'Every country is determined to have the biggest guns. They don't make those big guns for ornaments, they make them to be used. If we don't find understanding in this world, all mankind is likely to be destroyed.

'What the white man calls civilisation has a lot of foolishness about it. It needs a foundation of Indian common sense. You white people rush about madly to make money you'll never live long enough to spend, using up the forests, soil and natural fuels as though another generation won't need them, and all the time talking about a better world while making bigger bombs to blow up the one you've got. My people took a few scalps from their enemies but were never guilty of scalping nature's resources from an entire country.

'The Great Spirit, my God, desires that men live together in tolerant understanding, as the various species of trees growing side by side along the Bow River. There are black poplars, red willows, white ash and others. They grow together without hatred.

'It is part of the Great Spirit's plan that every person should be a searcher for the truth and that everyone should have the same opportunities to find it. Doctrine and bias do not exist as far as the Great Spirit is concerned, and he will reward all those who truly search for him by revealing himself in some way.

'I have searched all my life and found the Great Spirit's work in almost everything: the sun, moon, trees, wind and mountains. Sometimes I approach him through these things, for I have a true belief in the supreme being and a stronger faith than most white men who call us Indians, pagans and savages.

'Nature is the book of that great power which the white man calls God and which we call the Great Spirit. What difference does a name make? We have none of your denominations to split us, to introduce hatred in the name of religion.

'We do not have a place called Hell, for nobody can find the Great Spirit through fear. He would not choose to inflict everlasting torture on man as a punishment for not following his religion. Neither would he restrict his truth to a few favoured humans, allowing the others to remain in eternal darkness. The Great Spirit gives all humans in all lands an equal chance of enlightenment. Perhaps that explains why nearly all the world's religions have points in common, like charity, forgiveness and belief in a life after death.

'My people have been searching for the truth for generations, and they continue to find it. We have no man-made guides to "right living". Nature is our guide.

Nature is still my Bible and I will keep studying it until the day I die.'

The reverend doctor had years ago hoped to convince his adopted son to convert to Methodism. But when met with ardour such as this, he knew such hopes had always been futile. Now, in his new posting in Manitoba, Maclean reflected on Walking Buffalo's words in relation to the province's ongoing educational strife.

'There are many white men who mean well. The MacDougalls are my greatest white friends, you are my adoptive father, but you all underestimate the Indian faith. It was said that Christianity and education were the two bridges over which Indians would travel to be rescued from the abyss of ignorance and paganism, but the Indians were not, and are not, wholly convinced. "Never mind," said the white man, the Indians would have to change, because the white man said so.

'You missionaries first introduced classroom education, and the federal government was quite content to leave the matter of schools to the different churches. What happened then was a race to win the Indians regardless of whether it was the right thing for them.

'Displaying more religious zeal than understanding, those churches considered their chief purpose to be the conversion of so called heathens to whatever their own personal denomination. It was a recipe for disaster.

'I was lucky. Thanks to you and MacDougall, I had the opportunity of a good education. But although Indians may be ready for integrated education, the white people are not. We want schools on our land so that Indian boys and girls will not have to live in an unsympathetic community. And we want teachers who run those schools to understand and listen to us Indians, not preach and indoctrinate.

'You are a man who listens, John. You respect the Indian's faith in the Great Spirit. You should not feel a failure for that, you should feel great pride.'

George spoke so much good sense, but sadly, his points were not only relevant to the situation in Manitoba in 1896, but also to the creation of Indian residential schools in 1884.

These establishments were government-sponsored religious schools created to remove indigenous children from the influence of their own culture and assimilate them into the dominant Canadian culture. Walking Buffalo strongly disapproved.

'We are Indians! And proud to be Indians. I've said it before and I'll say it again, the schools should be on our land and they should support our culture, not try and dismember it.'

The reverend doctor, too, feared the worst, and both men's concerns were vindicated. The residential schools became an unmitigated disaster.

Each school was provided with an allowance per student, which led to overcrowding and the spread of disease within the institutions. In 1907 Doctor Peter Henderson Bryce, the chief medical officer responsible for Indian Affairs, revealed that indigenous children in the schools were dying at alarming rates. It wasn't until a year after he left office in 1921 that he was able to publish 'The Story of a National Crime', exposing the government's suppression of information on the health of enrolled indigenous children, and decrying 'a criminal disregard for the treaty pledge'.

Only in the 1960s were most residential schools finally closed, with thousands of indigenous children then placed in foster care or adoption homes, often with non-indigenous families.

It took until 2008 for Prime Minister Stephen Harper to offer a public apology on behalf of the government of Canada. A Truth and Reconciliation Commission was established, and school survivors interviewed, revealing alarming levels of abuse on many levels.

For Christmas 1898, the whole Maclean family descended on the Barker family home in Guelph. At the time, Walter was fifteen years of age, Owie fourteen, Alice thirteen, Bertie eight, Evelyn two and Willard just a twinkle in the reverend's forty seven-year-old eye. Annie and some of the children fell ill over the festive period and needed some weeks of convalescence leading into the new year. It gave the reverend doctor an opportunity to visit some of his old stomping grounds and meet old friends. He was invited to preach and enjoyed giving sermons from pulpits that were familiar to him. Walter, who was not suffering from the same influenza as the rest of the family, went with his father on a number of occasions.

After one such service, Maclean's old friends the McCraes were keen to catch up with him. Lieutenant Colonel David McCrae was the son of a Scottish immigrant, and he and his wife, Janet, and their three young children, Thomas, John and Geills, used to sit in church and listen to the young man from Glasgow when he was a mere lay preacher.

Maclean was now a reverend doctor, had undertaken a mission and was a published author to boot. The McCraes wanted to know all about it and invited John and Walter back to their house for some refreshment, which they were only too glad to accept. The McCraes explained that their son John, whom Maclean had last seen eighteen years before, was coming for lunch. Thomas was a promising doctor in Baltimore, and Geills had married a lawyer and was living in Winnipeg.

Like his brother, John McCrae had followed the medical route, although initially he had completed a Bachelor of Arts degree in English at the University of Toronto, where his interest in writing and poetry was established. His studies had been interrupted due to recurring problems with asthma, but in 1894 he published his first poems whilst teaching English and Maths at the Ontario Agricultural College in Guelph.

Ultimately, though, the draw of science proved too strong, and he was awarded a scholarship to study medicine; now, at the age of twenty-six, he was undertaking his first residency at Toronto General Hospital.

When Maclean was introduced to John McCrae, the reverend doctor noted that McCrae was a man of real charisma who could seemingly turn his hand to anything. There followed a fascinating lunchtime that went on far longer than anyone had expected, as they chatted about Maclean's mission, his family and his writing, which had included some poetry.

The McCraes fully involved the young Walter in the conversation and, as a teenager with keen social awareness, he thoroughly enjoyed the range of the debate. John McCrae talked of his love for the army and told of his training as an artilleryman at the Royal Military College of Canada in Kingston, Ontario. Maclean watched his son's eyes open wide with desire at the concept of trying to combine a medical career and the army.

The reverend doctor was keen to hear some of McCrae's poetry before they left, and he was happy to oblige.

'In light of your experiences in frontier towns and on the reserve,' he said, opening his published work, 'this might be appropriate. It's called "Anarchy".

' "I saw a city filled with lust and shame,
Where men, like wolves, slunk through the grim half-light;
And sudden, in the midst of it, there came
One who spoke boldly for the cause of Right.
And speaking, fell before that brutish race
Like some wren that shrieking eagles tear,
While brute Dishonour, with her bloodless face
Stood by and smote his lips that moved in prayer.
"Speak not of God! In centuries that word
Hath not been uttered! Our own king are we."
And God stretched forth his finger as He heard
And o'er it cast a thousand leagues of sea." '

McCrae's recital was clear, precise, almost matter-of fact. He decried people who read poetry in a melodramatic way. The poem had a profound effect on Maclean. He had written many stanzas, but none matched the quality of those he'd just heard. He was genuinely impressed and so too was Walter.

McCrae offered the book to the young Maclean, explaining that his father had bought so many copies that 'You cannot escape, Walter. Almost everyone who comes to the house goes away with a book of my poetry. I hope to meet you again one day.' McCrae would get his wish, but in fateful circumstances.

As they walked the mile or so back across Guelph to the Barker's home, Maclean and his son chatted. The reverend doctor liked the idea of Walter studying medicine, but he was less keen on him combining it with a career in the army. He saw world politics as volatile, foreseeing that growing international bellicosity would lead to conflict, war and death.

Maclean did not have to wait long to be proven right. Shortly after Willard, or WG, was born in Neepawa, Canada sent a battalion of volunteers to support the British in the Boer War (1899-1902), appeasing the pro-Empire Canadians pressuring the government to do something. It was the first time this young country had sent an official dispatch of troops abroad to fight.

John McCrae was amongst the seven thousand Canadians, including twelve women nurses, who fought in the war. He served as a lieutenant in the Canadian Field Artillery and was not amongst the 2,067 who were killed. The government claimed that their first overseas expedition had not set a precedent for involvement in further conflicts. Maclean did not believe them.

After making it home, McCrae worked at the Royal Victoria Hospital before heading to England to study and take his exams to become a member of the Royal College of Physicians.

Meanwhile, the reverend doctor had been appointed

editor of the Wesleyan, a publication that served the Methodist Church and had offices in Halifax. John moved his family the not inconsiderable distance of 2,222 miles (3,575 km) from Carman, Manitoba, where they had spent a year.

Moving from the dry, cold climate of Manitoba to the dampness of the Atlantic Coast brought on six months of severe illness for Annie, during which time she came perilously close to death. She spent much of that time in the hospital at Halifax, where Walter had enrolled to study medicine. Despite her frailty, Annie was delighted the physician looking after her was a woman: Doctor Susan Hearts, daughter of a local reverend. Annie's sisters would have been proud that a female doctor did so much to keep a member of their sisterhood alive.

This posting in Halifax was the first occasion Maclean did not have responsibility for developing a congregation. It felt strange. He published another book and was in demand to speak at church organisations, to whom the story of the missionary fields in the west was new and interesting.

The kindness and sincerity of the Nova Scotians endeared them to the Macleans, but Annie continued to struggle with the climate, and once Walter had qualified as a doctor from Victoria General Hospital, Maclean moved back, first to Morden, Manitoba for five years, and then in 1911, at the age of sixty, to Bethel Mission in North Winnipeg.

Walter, meanwhile, pursued his dream of following in the footsteps of John McCrae, attending the Royal Military College of Canada, before getting his first medical post back where he'd studied. He had loved his time in Halifax and jumped at the chance of returning. But as he went to work in mid-April 1912, he had no way of knowing how busy his first weeks there would be.

News filtered through of a human tragedy on a colossal scale. The *Titanic* had sunk some 700 miles east of Halifax with the loss of over 1500 lives. RMS *Carpathia* picked up the 700 or so survivors and took them to New York, leaving behind a seascape dotted with flotsam, icebergs and human remains. The unenviable task of dealing with the watery grave fell to the nearest port, which was Halifax.

White Star Line, the company which owned the *Titanic*, chartered several cable ships, ordinarily used to repair transatlantic telegraph cables, to go out, loaded with coffins, ice, embalming fluid and body bags, to retrieve the dead. As the ships returned with their grisly cargo, the city approached its job with stoic professionalism.

Halifax became the *Titanic*'s coroner, undertaker and mourner. Walter was involved in gathering and identifying the dead at the port's curling rink, which became a makeshift morgue. The bodies were dealt with and buried with great diligence and respect.

Of the reverend doctor's other children, Owie was working for the Canadian Pacific Railway, Bertie had joined the Mounted Police Force, whilst Alice had fallen for one of Bertie's colleagues and was engaged to be married. It would soon be only Evelyn and WG living at home.

Maclean's 1911 posting was to a small struggling

church in Winnipeg, Bethel Church on Alexander Avenue West. The district was rapidly changing, populated by a majority of poor white folk struggling to find work. The church was unable to support itself and labouring under a heavy mortgage.

John was now sixty, and Annie not much less, and with Evelyn, fifteen and Willard, twelve, in tow, they had a job on their hands. The only way forward was to set about making the church a centre of the community and to give their congregation a sense of worth and self-esteem.

John involved town planners to see what help politicians could offer, and the church became a hub of clubs and social activities that meant it was open every day. Within a year they had a Sunday School and a free concert every Saturday night that thronged with numbers regularly over seven hundred. They got the church finances in order and had to rent adjacent buildings to accommodate the numbers of people attending. In time, their venture was re-named Maclean Mission to acknowledge how the couple had rejuvenated the area.

But all the time, John was keeping a close eye on international affairs; he had three sons of fighting age and he feared for them should war break out. When Britain declared war on Germany at the start of World War One, Canada, as a Dominion within the British Empire, was at war as well. Within a day Canada had also declared war, exerting its importance as its own nation state.

Patriotic fervour gripped pro-Empire towns and cities. There were military parades with bunting and

Union Jack flags everywhere. Concerts and rallies took place, and shop windows displayed photographs of King George V and Lord Kitchener, the British Secretary of State for War. Photographs would soon be followed by war maps, allowing passers-by to keep informed of activity on the Western Front.

It worried the reverend doctor that the war was being romanticised. He foresaw a bloody mess. But before he could be proved right, there was a happier matter to attend to. Walter proposed to his sweetheart Allie (an abbreviation of Alison) and they took some time off to travel to Winnipeg and get married.

In the Maclean tradition, it was an informal occasion. John loved the fact that the reception was held in their house, guests spilling into the garden, sharing the food they had brought to celebrate the couple's union.

Within a few months, the first Canadian troops sailed for England, and Walter, Owie and Bertie were amongst them. Willard was still too young to fight. Maclean wondered how many, if any, of his sons would return.

Walter, as an army surgeon, was split up from his brothers and posted to the front to treat the many wounded casualties. He recognised the major of the First Brigade of Canadian Field Artillery, which he was serving with, as the man who had inspired him as a fifteen-year-old, John McCrae. In the seventeen intervening years, Walter had grown into a man, and so he introduced himself to McCrae, who was delighted to be reacquainted, although sad it was in such circumstances.

On May 2nd, 1915, McCrae was treating wounded soldiers from the Second Battle of Ypres when news reached him that his great friend, Lieutenant Alexis Helmer, had taken a direct hit from an eight-inch German shell and was dead.

The chaplain had been called to perform some burials at a nearby battalion, and so it fell to John McCrae to conduct the burial service for his friend. It affected him deeply. The following day he was sitting on the back of a medical field ambulance near an advance dressing post. The summer soil had been fertilised by thousands of corpses from the First Battle of Ypres, and there was a vast sheet of rich, scarlet poppies that covered the ground, as though the earth was disclosing her blood and refusing to cover the slain. It was where, with a pencil and a piece of paper, McCrae wrote his first draft of 'In Flanders Fields':

'In Flanders fields the poppies blow
Between the crosses, row on row,
That mark our place; and in the sky
The larks, still bravely singing, fly
Scarce heard amid the guns below

We are the Dead. Short days ago
We lived, fell down, saw sunset glow,
Loved and were loved, and now we lie
In Flanders fields.
Take up our quarrel with the foe:

To you from failing hands we throw
The torch; be yours to hold it high.

If ye break faith with us who die
We shall not sleep, though poppies grow
In Flanders fields.'

The Spectator magazine rejected the poem when McCrae sent it to them, but it was published in *Punch* on December 8th, 1915, anonymously until such time as they recognised him as the author. The verses quickly became one of the most popular poems of the war, used in numerous fund-raising campaigns.

Walter wrote home to tell his parents of his time with John McCrae, as he knew it would please them and that they would be moved by the poem.

Sadly, on January 28th, 1918, while in command of a third Canadian General Hospital, which he had established near Boulogne-sur-Mer, McCrae died of pneumonia. He was buried with full military honours, the flag-draped coffin and cortège preceded by McCrae's black charger, Bonfire. The two had been together from Valcartier, Quebec, and were inseparable. For the last farewell they reversed the Lieutenant Colonel's boots in Bonfire's stirrups.

As the war progressed the government was unprepared for the large number of Canadian casualties but eventually developed a system of informing families by telegram when their kin were wounded, taken prisoner or had died. Names were not to be released to the press until after close relatives had been informed.

Mistakes did occur, but most of the time the sad news carried by the missives was true. As the war dragged on, no news was good news, and families who had members fighting came to dread the appearance of the telegram boy on their street. Visitors to a house called out when they arrived – nobody knocked the door anymore.

John Maclean was keeping himself busy, although he couldn't help but look in the shop windows every day to stay abreast of military movements. Letters from his sons kept landing regularly and reassuringly on their door mat, and Willard's academic progress was a source of satisfaction. He was following in Walter's footsteps, a keen student with an interest in studying medicine.

Whilst in Halifax, Maclean had written the biography of a friend, *The Life of William Anderson Black*. At seventy-six, Black had been the oldest person ever elected to the Canadian House of Commons, and he was an example of what could be achieved in one's later years. The book had first been published in 1907, as a standalone volume, and though it was now ten years later, the reverend doctor hoped his Halifax publishers would consider it the basis of a new book about the key personnel who had created the nation of Canada.

Maclean included the stories of both indigenous and white men, calling the work *The Vanguards of Canada*. However, his Halifax publishers, who were struggling financially, dithered on whether or not to go to print. Maclean resolved to go and see them in person. It was a long way east, but he always enjoyed visiting the area, and if he went in early December, he would be back in time to prepare for Christmas in the community. He would be unable to visit his daughter-in-law, Allie, as she had sailed to France to spend some time with her husband, who had been granted some leave. However, he could instead stay with his Haligonian friend William Black.

In April 1917, the Canadians had been tasked with capturing the strategically important Vimy Ridge, which they'd done with typical efficiency, with Walter in the medical backup team supporting the troops. General Douglas Haig, commander of British armies in Europe, planned to capitalise on this victory by pushing through the German front lines in Belgium, advancing to the coast and liberating the ports. British prime minister David Lloyd George was sceptical of the scheme, but nonetheless it was approved by the British war cabinet.

Nothing strategic was ever put in personal letters, for fear of information being intercepted by spies, but when the Third Battle of Ypres started in July 1917, the reverend doctor guessed that the Canadian Expeditionary Force of about 100,000 would be involved in some way. The campaign became better known as the Battle of Passchendaele.

A two-week artillery bombardment of German encampments on the ridges around Ypres was aimed at paving the way for advances on the ground. The Canadians were not involved in this initial blitz; instead they were preparing to attack Lens to try and draw the Germans out and weaken them in Ypres.

The first and second battles of Ypres had destroyed the drainage systems that channelled rainwater from the fields. The terrain was now a quagmire of mud, with torrential rain falling into millions of craters caused by the continuous shelling campaign. In August, hundreds of thousands of soldiers on opposing sides attacked and counter-attacked across an apocalyptic wasteland. Tens of thousands died, but Haig still refused to halt the offensive, which had made little or no progress.

By October, Haig decided to turn to the Canadians for help. Lieutenant General Arthur Currie, the Canadian Corps' commander, objected to the recklessness of Haig's plan but had no real option other than to comply. He ordered four divisions to the land around Passchendaele village.

In Winnipeg, the number of volunteers was down to a trickle, just as in many towns and cities across the country. The war seemed to be in stalemate, with no end in sight and many reported casualties. It led swiftly to the Military Service Act, which enforced conscription.

Every day, as John Maclean walked to work, he would pass a general store that displayed a big map of the Western Front. One October morning, he noticed the shop owner rearranging four large arrows to centre on Ypres. The man waved cheerily, glad that someone was appreciating his work. John tried to raise a smile but deep down he was worried. His sons had lasted the war this long, but the concentration of Canadian troops in one area portended a major offensive.

Owie and Albert were fortunately not involved in this attack. Walter, however, was stationed slightly behind the front lines, ready to treat the many expected casualties. The danger of errant shells was constant.

Even the terrain of the battlefield was treacherous. Soldiers and pack horses laden with supplies and the dead had to pick their way across narrow 'duck walk' tracks that wound around the craters. If you slipped into a crater, that was often it – you drowned.

Amongst these conditions the troops readied themselves for the attack, which was due to start on October 26th. For two weeks after that date the divisions took it in turns to assault Passchendaele Ridge. They made about 200 metres each day but suffered heavy losses. On October 30th, Canada lost almost all its junior officers from Princess Patricia's Canadian Light Infantry in just one hour's fighting.

It became impossible to tell where the front line separating Canadian and German positions actually was, and soldiers became lost in the horrifying mud. Whale oil was distributed to rub on soldier's feet to prevent 'trench-foot'. As one infantryman recorded: 'The enemy and ourselves are in the self-same muck, degradation and horror to such a point nobody cares anymore about anything, only getting out of this, and the only way out is by death or wounding. All of us welcome either.'

Walter and the medical services did their best in these very trying circumstances, and on November 6th, the Canadians launched their third attack on Passchendaele Ridge and succeeded in capturing it. Over the entire battle, more than four thousand Canadians were killed and twelve thousand wounded.

But despite it all, they had succeeded once again, although in a battle they were not truly convinced was worth fighting. Nine Victoria Crosses, the British Empire's highest award for bravery, were awarded to Canadians after this battle. Walter had come through with his life. It was something to be grateful for; three days later corpses still passed their tent, where they desperately treated horrific injuries, trying to keep their patients alive.

Then an order came through for a fourth assault on the remaining high ground east of Ypres. The campaign they had thought won was not over yet. But it would take only one more day of fighting, hopefully, to conclude an offensive that had lasted for over four months.

Walter completed a twelve-hour shift before grabbing some sleep. He was due back on duty that evening. On waking, he shaved with cold water and dressed before starting the walk to the hospital tents. He thought of the time off he'd spent in France with Allie just recently.

They had spent a long weekend amongst the cafés and bars of France's capital, staying in the Rive Gauche area, the Left Bank, known as the artistic quarter. They had talked of starting a family as soon as the war was over. Neither of them had been abroad before, and in this brief respite from the horrors of the conflict, they could indulge their senses and dream of a fecund post war period.

Walter felt tired as he made his way to the field hospital but buoyed himself with these thoughts of the future. In his distraction, he got his boot stuck in a pothole and nearly fell. He laughed at his ineptitude to keep to the 'duck walk' tracks. The rain had mercifully stopped, and it was a beautifully clear but chilly evening. In the viscous sludge, for a moment he couldn't move. He tried to spot some constellations in the sky as he extricated his boot from the mud. Was that a shooting star? Too close. There was a feeling of intense heat and then a searing bright light.

Invariably, John was the first up in the morning. He would make a pot of tea, even if he was the only one who would drink it, the others preferring coffee. Quite often Willard would pour himself a cup and never touch a drop; he would just chat with his father, who he affectionately called 'the old boy'.

They would lean against the kitchen sides and natter away, Evelyn imploring them to sit at the table, but it was one of John Maclean's mantras that once he was up for the day, he wouldn't sit down until a task had been completed.

Annie joined them, rubbing her knuckle where, many years ago now, she'd had her finger amputated. John ushered her forward and put his gnarled paws around his wife's tiny hands, blowing through a tiny porthole between his fingers and thumbs, the blast of hot air easing the aching in her joints. Evelyn put two eggs onto boil, one for her and one for her mother, and enlisted her father's help to time them with his pocket watch.

John loved this hive of family activity and chatted on merrily with WG about his lectures. Evelyn deplored the accuracy of his timekeeping, to which he replied, 'I'm on the case, lass. On the case. D'you ken?'

John had long brought Scottish colloquialisms into conversations with his children, reminding them of their heritage and the beauty of language, and celebrating the diversity of procreation.

' "Lass" is a girl, Evelyn. "Ken" means "know".'

John knew that she had heard this a thousand times, and she would hear it again now for his amusement.

Then: 'Rat-a-tat-tat.' A knock on the front door.

They all looked at each other, each one breaking into a cold sweat. Nobody moved, hoping against hope the telegram boy had the wrong address.

'Rat-a-tat-tat!'

The noise echoed throughout the house as John stepped forward to attend to matters. He had walked this walk before. Twenty-seven years had passed since Richie's death, but the journey to tell Annie the news had scarred John forever. Nobody else moved. They just stood there, as if frozen in time. They prayed as they heard John accept the telegram and close the door.

He walked slowly into the kitchen with a desolate look on his face. His eyes were filled with tears as he read.

'It is with deep regret that I have to inform you of the sad death of Major W.L. Maclean of the 1st Canadian C.C.S., B.E.F. France on the 10th November, 1917...'

John's voice started strongly but cracked as easily as an eggshell when he got to the word 'death'. Willard and Evelyn had never known Richie or Dorothy, but the wound of their passing opened up once more as their parents wept openly, standing in the kitchen.

As he regained some of his composure, John

offered prayers for Walter, trying to come to terms with the news. It would be another two weeks before letters of condolence started arriving from overseas.

'November 10, 1917
My Dear Dr and Mrs Maclean,

Long before this letter reaches you the authorities will have notified you of the death of your son Major W.L. Maclean. He was my second in command and nobody ever had a more faithful friend and companion.

He was a wonderful surgeon, being rated at Head Quarters as one of the best on the whole front. It is inexpressibly sad that a career giving such promise should have been cut short by an enemy bombing a hospital when they had lost the battle.

In the course of a few weeks he was going to be promoted to Lieutenant Colonel and command this unit as I am taking another post. We have been together nearly two years and I miss him more than I would a brother.

He was just coming into the hospital when a bomb fell beside him at 7 p.m. (the 9th) and he lived 'til 02.15 a.m. this morning the 10th. He wished me to write to you and to say he had done what he could and he sent his love to his father and mother, brothers and sisters.

Walter had a 'through and through' wound of the chest, a broken arm and a flesh would of the hip. He suffered from shock but had very little pain. Captain Leckum, a splendid surgeon did everything possible but alas in vain.

I, and all the unit are very upset by his untimely

end and his place can never be filled. His loss to the Canadian Medical Service is a very serious one as he was the best surgeon in our service. We feel the emptiness of his chair in our midst.

We, who lived and worked with him recognised his ability and faithfulness to duty that won our respect and admiration but it was his modest manliness and genial nature that claimed our love.

I have written to his poor wife, they had just finished a leave in Paris and enjoyed themselves very much. I am glad he was able to spend time with Allie, and she can always look back to his leave and remember him as she saw him last.

It was only yesterday he was talking to me about you and saying he must help you educate his youngest brother Willard. He wanted to take him to practice with himself when he had qualified.

We shall bury Walter tomorrow at 11 a.m. on the eleventh day, of the eleventh month, 1917. I have just sent for a casket and I shall have the site well marked, so if after the war you are able to get out here, you will experience no difficulty in finding his last resting place.

Six of our sergeants will carry the coffin on their shoulders, followed by the Officers of our unit and those of the surrounding Casualty Clearing Stations. Some men of a Scotch Regiment whose lives he saved have also expressed a desire to attend the funeral.

I feel deeply for you and your wife and for Major Maclean's wife, we all feel here that we have lost a strong personal friend. I am sorry I cannot write you any more but you can realise how dreadfully upset I am at present.

Sincerely yours
C.H. Dickson
Lieutenant-Colonel, C.A.M.C.
O.C. in Canadian Casualty Clearing Station'

Too devastated to put any effort into getting his new book published, John sent a telegram to his publishers in Halifax, postponing their meeting. He also sent a telegram apologising to his friend William Black, with whom he had been due to stay during negotiations. Walter's widow was due back in Halifax in early December, and John revised his plans to coincide his visit with her return.

Aside from losing her husband, Allie now had to decide what to do with the apartment they had been renting. John wanted to take Annie with him to try and give her as much moral support as possible. It would probably mean staying for a week or so in a month that was one of the busiest in the church's calendar.

John organised people to deputise for him and sent a telegram to Allie informing her of their plans. All they needed was a reply from their daughter-in-law to action everything. However, even at the best of times, Atlantic sea crossings depended very much on the weather, and now there was also the threat of German U-boats. A safe passage was never guaranteed. RMS *Lusitania*, a British ocean liner, had been torpedoed on the 7th May 1915, with the deaths of 1,198 civilian passengers and crew.

John had been to the telegram operator to explain no more telegrams were to be delivered to the house under any circumstances. He or Willard would check with the telegram company on a daily basis, rather than put the family through the shock of an unexpected delivery again. It was no extra burden for John, as it was on his route to and from work. Invariably he would pick up a newspaper in the shop next door at the same time.

On the morning of the 8th December 1917, Maclean picked up his paper and, without looking at it, folded it and put it under his arm. As he left the shop, his eye was caught by the billboard outside the newsagent. The headline of the *Winnipeg Free Press* was just two words emboldened in large print: 'HALIFAX EXPLOSION'. He stopped in his tracks, his mind racing.

The Halifax explosion made for depressing reading. The SS *Mont-Blanc*, a French cargo ship, had been fully laden with TNT explosives, picric acid, gun cotton and the highly flammable fuel benzole. Before the war, ships carrying dangerous cargo had not been allowed into Halifax's harbour, but the risks posed by German submarines had resulted in a relaxation of regulations.

The Norwegian ship SS *Imo* was en route to New York, where it was to take on relief supplies for Belgium. It was heading out of port while the *Mont-Blanc* was coming in, both ships negotiating a tricky strait called the Narrows. The two vessels had river pilots, and the rules of the Bedford Basin were that ships had to pass port to port at a restricted speed of five knots.

For a variety of reasons that didn't happen. Both ships were occupying the same channel, and although they had both cut their engines, and in fact the SS *Imo* was in reverse, there was a light collision between the two. But the real problem occurred when the ships uncoupled. Having punctured a hole high up in the *Mont Blanc*'s hull, the *Imo* toppled barrels of benzole, and in the disengagement, sparks ignited vapours from the spillage.

A fire started at the water line, quickly travelling up the side of the ship as benzole spewed out from the crushed drums on *Mont-Blanc*'s decks. The fire soon became uncontrollable, and the captain ordered everyone to abandon ship, fearing an explosion.

The frantic crew of the *Mont-Blanc* shouted warnings from their two lifeboats as they desperately tried to row away, but they could not be heard above the noise and confusion. The abandoned ship continued to drift and beached at Pier Six, near the start of Richmond Street, right in the heart of the harbour.

For twenty minutes, the SS *Mont-Blanc* burned. A whaler and a tug approached to see if they could tow the stricken vessel away. They were not aware of the cargo on board. Neither were the school children walking to school, the growing number of people gathering on the harbour side, or the many standing at the windows of their homes and businesses, watching the spectacular fire.

At 9.05 am the *Mont-Blanc*'s highly explosive cargo detonated. The ship was completely blown apart. White hot shards of iron fell down from the sky, *Mont Blanc*'s forward ninety-millimetre gun landing three and half miles away, and the shank of her anchor, weighing half-a-ton, two miles away.

The shockwaves travelled through the earth at nearly

twenty-three times the speed of sound. Everything within a half mile radius was levelled. A pressure wave snapped trees, twisted iron rails and demolished buildings. The blast was the largest manmade explosion prior to the development of nuclear weapons.

The volume of vaporised water exposed the harbour floor, and a tsunami was formed by the water surging to fill the void. The wave rose 60 feet (18 metres) above the high-water mark in the harbour.

Hundreds of people watching the fire from homes or businesses were blinded as shards of glass fired in all directions. Hardly a window in Halifax was left unbroken. Stoves and lamps overturned by the blast sparked fires throughout the town. Entire blocks were caught up in the inferno, with trapped residents inside.

Vince Coleman, who worked at the railway yard, knew of the ship's cargo and, upon hearing of the collision, hurried to leave. But realising there were trains due in, he returned to his post and sent out a mayday. 'Hold up the trains. Ammunition ship afire in harbour and will explode. Guess this will be my last message. Goodbye, boys.' His message stopped all incoming trains around Halifax, saving countless lives but not his own.

Relief efforts the following day were hampered by a blizzard that covered Halifax in sixteen inches (forty-one centimetres) of snow. It put out the fires but knocked down the hastily re-erected telegraph poles and stranded trains coming to Halifax in snowdrifts. Halifax was isolated by the storm in a scene of unimaginable suffering.

Exact numbers of casualties were going to be impossible to collate, but the initial estimate was about

2,000 dead, 9,000 injured, 6,000 homeless, 25,000 with insufficient shelter. A group of indigenous Mi'kmaq people settled around Turtle Cove in the wider harbour were completely wiped out. Of the injured, nearly 6,000 had eye injuries. 1,630 homes were destroyed, 12,000 homes damaged.

As John took in the report, he realised that he should have been in Halifax to meet his publishers at the time of the explosion. There were so many unknowns it was difficult to formulate a plan, but the one thing the reverend doctor knew was that he had to be there.

Walter and Allie's apartment was in Dartmouth. They had been renting whilst saving to buy a house and had taken a cheaper place on the other side of the harbour. It was less densely populated than the port of Halifax but was still vulnerable, and if Allie had found her way home, if she wasn't dead, she was likely to be maimed or seriously injured.

Whether it was to find Allie's remains or to establish the facts, it was with clarity of thought that he returned home to explain to Annie what he thought they should do.

They boarded a train for Halifax the following day. Evelyn and Willard would hold fort whilst they were there, and the youngest Maclean would check with the telegram operator on a daily basis.

When John and Annie finally got to their destination, they could not believe the utter devastation they were witness to. The Halifax Relief Commission had already been hastily set up to organise medical relief, transportation, food, shelter and to cover medical and funeral costs for victims. The military was involved in clearing the streets, and an American steamship, *Old Colony*, had docked to serve as a hospital ship, staffed by doctors and orderlies from British and American navy vessels that had also arrived in the harbour.

A mortuary committee was formed at the city hall, which, despite having its windows blown out, was otherwise untouched. A school was commandeered to act as morgue, and a constant stream of trucks and wagons arrived with bodies. A system to carefully number and describe the bodies was implemented, based on the programme developed to identify *Titanic* victims in 1912.

John and Annie called first at the home of their old friend William Black, who lived in a residential area relatively far away from the harbour. Houses such as his, made from stone and brick, had fared better than the town's wooden structures. They were greeted by his wife, who was overjoyed to see them. She explained that her husband was in town co-ordinating the delivery of aid from Boston down the coast, where he had good links. The Macleans dropped off their bags and set off to discover what had become of their daughter-in-law.

Snow was still hampering the relief effort, but John and Annie laboriously made their way to Dartmouth, where their son and his wife had lived. It was separated from the blast by the width of the harbour but had still suffered heavy damage. The Macleans struggled to get their bearings amid the carnage, but they eventually found the apartment block they were looking for – or rather, where it should have been. The Macleans checked and double checked, but eventually they had to admit to themselves that this was where Walter and

Allie had lived. It was now merely rubble and splintered wood.

To the morgue, where there was no record of Mrs Alison Maclean. John knew, though, that there would be huge numbers of people missing or unidentifiable. Next, to the shipping company, where their efforts were like trying to find a needle in a haystack. They didn't know where Allie had sailed from, the name of the ship or the date it had set off. All they did know was that she was due back in Halifax in early December. Ships had been diverted from the damaged port, and their only hope was that Annie had docked elsewhere and was somehow making her way home.

It was an interminable waiting game with stakes of the highest order. The Macleans told the Blacks that they would stay to the end of the week and then they would have to make their way home. Privately, John realised that people close to the blast would have been vaporised, and that authorities would never know the names of some people who perished or exactly how many had died.

From his days on the Blood reservation, coping with tragedy had been a part of Maclean's life. Allie had lost both parents to smallpox over five years ago, and John had helped counsel her through her suffering. From then, John and Annie had assumed greater responsibility for their daughter-in-law, becoming almost surrogate parents.

The reverend doctor relied on a process of talk, prayer and song to help people deal with their bereavement. But it was easier to come to terms with loss if you had a body to either bury or cremate. Even he was struggling to come to terms with the anguish of not knowing whether Allie was dead or alive, or indeed, if they would ever know.

Telegrams had only been harbingers of doom as far as the reverend was concerned but as William Black handed the crackly paper to him, he had the faintest of smiles.

'Allie safe and well. Been diverted. Now heading to Halifax. Check incoming trains. Willard.'

It was the good news John and Annie had been praying for. After the events of recent weeks, it felt as though the message had been heaven sent. William Black accompanied his friend to the station whilst Annie and Susan, William's wife, readied a bedroom.

Sure enough, as they scanned everyone disembarking from the civilian trains that rolled in with the freight trains carrying aid, there stepped the visage they were looking for. It was a bittersweet moment, for as much as John was elated to see Allie, it was the first time they had met since Walter's death, and it brought suppressed emotions to the fore.

Allie had not recovered particularly well from the Atlantic crossing and during the evening needed to use the bathroom regularly. When she was violently sick the following morning, John feared she had picked up an illness on board. But Susan thought otherwise and looked knowingly at Annie as they had breakfast. Annie nodded in agreement. She had also had the same thought.

Susan brought out her calendar and counted back the weeks to the long weekend of leave Walter and Allie had enjoyed in Paris. It was only six weeks ago; they felt sure Allie was in the early stages of pregnancy. She was, and in July 1918, Margery was born.

During her pregnancy, Allie joined the Macleans in Winnipeg. It had been an easy decision to make: her town was in turmoil, her apartment destroyed, her parents and her husband had passed. But although Walter was dead, he had bequeathed Allie more than she could have ever hoped for, a daughter.

The Macleans were her family now, and she was ready to start a new life for herself, with people she cherished and who desperately wanted to be a part of her life.

Allie remained with them for a decade, until she was able to support her daughter by getting a job lecturing in English at the University of Manitoba. Margery thrived in the homeliness of the Maclean's Winnipeg home, and blossomed in her teens. Allie had to refuse a number of suitors. There would be time aplenty for that once Margery had left home.

But that was to prove sooner than Allie had planned, when Margery fell in love with one of her mother's students, a good looking chap called Jack Richards. They were married on 23rd May, 1939 with Allie's blessing. However, World War Two loomed large on the horizon, and sure enough, a short time after Britain had declared war on Germany in September 1939, so did Canada.

The appetite for war was not what it had been amongst the pro-Empire supporters in 1914, but nevertheless Canada entered the fray anxious to do its duty and to demonstrate the bravery it had exhibited in the First World War.

Jack enlisted in the Navy. It worried Allie and

Margery, but Jack, aware of the global danger of Hitler's Germany, and the more immediate threat posed by German U-boats in the North Atlantic, was fully committed to the war effort.

After eighteen months of the war, Jack was due to sail from Halifax on 23rd May, 1941, the day of his and Margery's second wedding anniversary. But before his departure, he was granted a few days leave. Allie booked Margery and Jack into the best hotel she could find, in the port she knew only too well. Planning to accompany Margery on the long journey, she found cheaper accommodation for herself. She wanted to give the young couple a bit of time and space, and she herself could revisit her and Walter's old haunts and think back over the good times they'd had.

It was the first time Allie had gone back to Halifax since her fateful return from Europe over twenty years before. It seemed strange that then she had been carrying Margery inside her, and she was now coming back with her daughter a fully fledged young woman.

They arrived before Jack docked, and so Allie was able to show Margery where her father had lived and worked. It was a cathartic visit, almost a pilgrimage, which Allie realised she might have made years ago, but now the time felt right. Allie was glad she'd made the journey. It was as though she was re-reading a chapter of her life that she would now hopefully be able to close. Much of the town, of course, had been rebuilt, and the metaphor for her own life was not lost on Allie. Having seen her daughter through to adulthood and marriage, it was time for her to move on too.

On their anniversary, Margery and Jack enjoyed

breakfast together, before Allie joined them and they walked to the quayside to see Jack's new ship, HMCS *Lévis*. She had been commissioned into the Royal Canadian Navy just a week ago in Quebec and had sailed up to Halifax to pick up supplies and more crew.

Jack was excited to be involved in convoy escort duties, part of the newly created Newfoundland Escort Force that was trying to protect allied shipping against the increasing threat of U-boat attack. The NEF would escort a convoy of ships to Iceland, where they would turn them over to British escorts, refuel and return to St John's with a westbound convoy.

Allie and Margery put on brave faces as they waved Jack off, before returning to the station to catch a train for the long journey east back to Winnipeg. Margery had seen for the first time where her parents had spent the formative years of their marriage, and she was keen to hear more snippets about her father. Allie indulged her daughter. The visit had brought back things she had completely forgotten about, and she spoke about facets of Walter's personality that were mirrored in Margery's own spirit and soul.

And there were things that Margery had inherited from her mother, too, so when one beautiful July morning, Allie heard her daughter retching, she knew instinctively it was morning sickness.

If it was history repeating itself in one sense, Allie prayed that the outcome would be different in another. But in mid-September, there came a knock at the door that made the hairs on the back of her neck stand up. In the way that you can recognise neighbours by the way they knock, both mother and daughter had a sense of foreboding at the loud, uniform and evenly spaced rat-tat-tat.

A smart, slightly older member of the military and a chaplain stood on the doorstep. Margery and Allie's worst fears were realised. HMCS *Lévis* had done one round trip to Iceland before joining convoy SC-44, when at 02.05 am, on 19th September 1941, she was torpedoed by a U-boat east of Cape Farewell, 120 miles off Greenland.

The explosion killed eighteen, amongst them one Jack Richards. Ninety-one crew were rescued, and as Margery wept, she prayed they'd made a mistake and that her husband was one of the survivors. But it wasn't to be, and when Hughie was born the following February, Margery, who had never met her father, knew the same fate had befallen her own son.

Chapter Sixteen

'To Willard Gladstone   August 10th 1918
Maclean Esq.,   Methodist
Pacific Avenue   Fresh Air Camp
Winnipeg   Gimli, Manitoba

'Dear Son,

You will receive this letter with the small gift of money enclosed on your nineteenth birthday. I wish I were able to give you ten times more than what it represents but 'the gift without the giver is bare' and although it does not amount to much in monetary value, it is more than I ever received from my father all my life, and it is given with your father's love.

    Now that you are nineteen years of age and I am no longer a young man, by the course of nature, I will gradually depend more upon you than ever and especially as you are the only one of my sons at home. You are so like our beloved Walter whose memory abides with me. His death seems to affect me sometimes that the tears will come when I am alone and I find myself weeping.

It is for you and Evelyn that I now desire to live, that I may see you both settled in life, for there cannot be many more years for me to remain in the ministry. You now mean more to me than ever and it is for you and me to help each other as far as we can and so make life one great success.

You have great ability and I am anxious that you fulfil your potential and become a great surgeon in much the same way as Walter, but above all else, I desire you to be a strong Christian and a good man. The greatest sacrifice I made on your behalf and the best legacy I can bequeath to my children is that I led an honourable life.

I am anxious to be honest before God and my fellow men so that my sons and daughters will ever remember their father as man who tried to do his duty. If God will prolong my life until I see you graduate I shall be content and then I shall be ready to step aside and take a little rest before I am called home.

Among my richest treasures is a letter Walter sent me from the front thanking your mother and I for what we had done for him. When he had started earning for himself he expressed his surprise and gratitude as he said he could not understand how we were able to give all you children such a good education, and feed you all so well, on the small salary that I received. The largest credit is due to your mother for her good management of the home. For what she has been able to achieve is truly remarkable.

I am naturally proud of our family and commend them to God. And now I pray that the Lord will help you to be ambitious in your profession and will grant you grace that you may live a real Christian life, helping your fellows and glorifying God as a great surgeon.

This is my highest and best wish for you on your nineteenth birthday,

Your affectionate father,
John Maclean'

Willard was greatly touched by his dad's letter but worried that, as his father edged ever closer to being a septuagenarian, his sense of his own mortality might itself precipitate his slowing up. Those thoughts were short-lived. John's spirits were rejuvenated by the entry of the United States into the First World War, thinking that the economic implications, and a fresh influx of troops, would foreshorten the war. It hadn't saved Walter, but it might mean Owie and Albert came home alive.

As his ministry was coming to an end, John started to look for other challenges to fill his time. The letter John had sent Willard was from Gimli, which the Methodist Church had set up in 1905 as an open air camp for disadvantaged urban children and their mothers to enjoy the great outdoors. This was something that the reverend doctor strongly believed in, and when visiting, he would always throw himself into the camp's activities with vim and vigour, despite his advancing years.

In 1918, he was appointed chief archivist of the Methodist Church of Canada (later the United Church) and librarian of Wesley College, part time jobs that he loved. Not to be outdone, Annie was, for a time, president of the Women's Missionary Society and member and often president of a whole host of other associations connected with the Church.

In 1918, on the eleventh day of the eleventh month, it was with mixed emotions that the Maclean household greeted the news of the Armistice's signing. Owie and Albert would return home alive, but with cruel irony the treaty also commemorated to the day the anniversary of Walter's burial.

Maclean was also worried about social tensions in Winnipeg. Owie and Albert returned home to their jobs, but others were not so lucky, with large numbers of immigrants filling their positions. Many found themselves unemployed and resentful. The soldiers also brought back a strain of Spanish flu, which quickly caused an epidemic. With a post war recession causing inflation, the melting pot of grievances just needed a little stir to cause widespread unrest.

The Bolsheviks' mobilisation in the Russian Revolution of 1917 was still recent history, so when more than thirty thousand workers walked out of work in May 1919, in what became known as the Winnipeg General Strike, the government were fully aware of the dangers.

After many arrests, deportations and incidents of violence, the strike effectively ended on June 21st, when the Riot Act was read and a group of Royal Canadian Mounted Police Officers charged a group of strikers. Two strikers were killed and at least thirty others injured, the day becoming known as 'Bloody Saturday', an event that polarised Canadian opinion.

For the next few days, the city was virtually under

military occupation, until on June 25th, 1919 the Central Strike Committee called off their action. The federal government, fearing that the strike would spread to other cities, ordered the senator of the region to mediate. Under political pressure, he settled in favour of the strikers and encouraged the city council to accept the employees' proposals. Although the workers' lot did not appreciably improve, many of the strike leaders would later be applauded as labour's champions and elected to serve in provincial and federal government, despite conviction for criminal charges.

Maclean was a reformist not a revolutionary. He had worked for nearly a decade amongst the poor in the city and could see things needed to change, but he did not condone the use of force. The strike worried him, and in typically proactive style, to try and broach the divide between immigrants and Canadians, he became Immigration Chaplain of the Methodist Church in Winnipeg; meanwhile, to better inform himself about legal matters, he also started a law degree at the University of Manitoba.

Willard was highly amused that on certain days of the week he travelled to university with his father beside him. There were nearly fifty years between them, but fresh study gave John a new lease of life. Of the two, it was he who asked the most questions of his professors. That said, Willard, too, thrived in the learned environment, and amongst his teachers, one in particular took a keen interest in him. His name was John C. Boileau Grant.

Willard was enraptured by Grant's clinical brilliance, which was allied to a clarity of expression delivered in a brogue similar to his father's. Grant inspired in Maclean a desire to travel to Grant's home city of Edinburgh, to get his Fellowship of the Royal College of Surgeons (FRCS), acknowledged to be one of the premiere fellowships in the world at the time.

Willard explained his plan to his father with such animation John knew that it would be foolhardy to try and deter him. Just as John had himself seized the opportunity to leave Scotland all those years ago, now his youngest son had the wanderlust to return to the land whence his father had come.

As soon he had qualified, Willard set sail, landing in Liverpool, where, finding nothing appropriate in Scotland, he got his first house job. In 1923, seeing an opening in Swansea, he moved to Wales and started work in a place that, unbeknownst to him, would entertain him for the rest of his life. The reason for such longevity was simple: professional and marital harmony.

On duty as a young house doctor one Sunday evening, W.G. was treating a well-dressed gentleman who he guessed was in his mid-fifties. Willard was sure the problem was gallstones, but his patient would have none of it, combatively testing the diagnosis. With assurance, Willard explained his reasoning to the patient and the young woman who had brought him in. Young Maclean's phlegmatic calm under questioning impressed the recent Member of Parliament for Swansea East, a certain David Matthews, and his daughter, Enid.

The young doctor was broad-shouldered and spoke with a Canadian accent that enchanted Enid. Although neither knew it, their meeting mirrored John and Annie's pre-courtship travails of decades past. But first there was her father to deal with.

'You mean to tell me, young woman,' said the vexed and impatient patient, 'that you believe this young doctor's diagnosis and not mine?'

'Yes!' spoke the defiant daughter. 'You are very good at many things, father, as well you know, but as far as medicine is concerned, you'd be better off leaving it to the professionals.'

'I need a second opinion, Enid.'

'Of course you do, father, but I have a feeling it will only confirm what the young Canadian says.'

'Why do you invest so much trust in this chap?'

'I don't, but his logic seems robust and well reasoned. And he amuses me, for he cannot say the word "orange". Well, he can, but when he described you as "the gentleman in the orange tie" he said "orange" with a long vowel in the middle. I laughed for an age, and he just stood there with a straight face, wondering what on earth he'd done to amuse me.'

Realising she was talking herself into trouble, Enid stopped abruptly.

'*Diddorol*,' David Matthews spoke in Welsh. 'Very interesting.'

David Matthews was a leading member of the civic community in Swansea. He had been a mayor of the city, a justice of the peace and twice chief magistrate. Alongside this, he owned a local tinplate company and was renowned for looking after the needs of his workforce and supporting the working man.

His social conscience was not only evident in the way he did business, but also in his political doctrine. Matthews was a strong supporter of David Lloyd

George, a fellow Welsh speaker and a good friend. Lloyd George had been prime minister from 1916 to 1922 and during his premiership had laid the foundations of the modern welfare state. But Lloyd George had lost the October 1922 election to the Conservative Party, led by Bonar Law, and David Matthews had stepped down as the Member of Parliament for Swansea East in the same year, with concerns about his health.

A senior consultant at Swansea General and Eye Hospital confirmed Willard's diagnosis of gallstones, and a few days later, Enid accompanied her father to the hospital to collect some test results.

'You seem quite keen to accompany me to the hospital these days, Enid,' he countered. 'Is there an ulterior motive perhaps? Let us seek him out. I would like to thank him for his treatment and admit that he was right and I was wrong.'

'Well, I will have to be there to witness such a rare event, father.'

'Oh, I'm sure you will, Enid. Now what was his name again?'

'Dr W.G. Maclean, I think.'

'You think! Your preciseness gives you away, my dear. You know full well what his name is.'

Enid gave in, smiling back at her mischievous father, and when they found the young doctor, she was as surprised as Willard when the medic was invited to dinner the coming Friday evening.

'Good looking fellow, Enid,' her father remarked on their way home. 'Strong jawline. Quite a quiet chap though. But I like his economy with words. He only says what needs to be said, and I get the feeling he doesn't suffer fools gladly. Anyway, we will soon find out his opinions, what with Lloyd George joining us. He feels another general election is in the offing, and he wants my views on tariffs and trade restrictions. I thought it only fair to warn Dr Maclean, and he didn't seem to bat an eyelid. I like his style.'

Willard was aware of the name David Lloyd George, and recalled he'd been prime minister, but that was as far as his knowledge went. Before the day of the dinner, he did a little research so as not to appear ignorant. He discovered that Lloyd George had been Chancellor of the Exchequer from 1908 to 1915, where his many achievements included the introduction of old age pensions, National Health Insurance, and unemployment insurance, paid for largely by taxes on high incomes and landowners.

In 1915, he had served as Minister of Munitions, successfully addressing the army's critical lack of ammunition. A year later, he took over from Asquith as prime minister, where his dynamic leadership played a key role in winning the First World War. At the end of the war his reputation stood at its peak, and he remained in power for the next four years. One commentator wrote that Lloyd George's energy, capacity for work and powers of recuperation were remarkable. He had an extraordinary memory and imagination and had mastered the art of being able to get to the root of the matter very quickly.

All in all, quite an imposing character to be dining with. But with the confidence of youth, Willard reasoned that his guilelessness when it came to British politics would allow him to ask direct questions without fear of retribution.

'Lloyd George, let me introduce a young Canadian to you,' said David Matthews, once Willard had arrived. The two politicians had been discussing tariff restrictions all afternoon and were in need of a rest. 'This is Dr W.G. Maclean, a promising medic, I feel.'

The two shook hands, Willard remembering what his father had always taught him: 'Look the person in the eye, always step forward, never backward and whatever you do, don't give a "wet leaf" handshake.'

'It's a pleasure to meet you, Lloyd George.'

'Not another talented Canadian over here,' the great statesman quipped to David Matthews, with reference to the Canadian-born Bonar Law, who had succeeded him as prime minister. He winked at Willard, tapping him on the shoulder to indicate he was jesting before resuming.

'W.G. – distinctive initials indeed.'

Willard looked quizzically at Lloyd George, and the politician continued.

'William Gladstone, one of this country's finest prime ministers and, nominally at least, a Liberal like myself. What a man he was! Head and shoulders above anyone else I have ever seen in the House of Commons. I did not like him much, but I admired his financial acumen, his support for devolving power and his ideas for a progressive party that listened to varying interests. He was by far and away the best Parliamentary speaker I have ever heard. But he hated Nonconformists, and Welsh Nonconformists in particular.'

'My father was a fan of his too,' Willard interjected.

'Hence my name, Willard Gladstone Maclean.

'Tell me about your father, young man.'

Willard explained about John's upbringing, experiences and achievements, which Lloyd George found fascinating.

'Sounds like your father was a Nonconformist himself,' he remarked. W.G, asking his ignorance be excused, questioned what was meant by Nonconformist. 'Well,' Lloyd George continued, 'it's a broad term that includes anyone who does not conform to the ways of the Church of England. Quite ridiculous really, but for many years, legally and socially, Nonconformists were restricted from many spheres of public life and employment. Thankfully, things have changed now, and we are not treated as badly. Some Nonconformists claim a devotion to hard work, temperance, frugality, integrity and upward mobility – which, having heard what you've said about your father, would definitely suit him. Tell me, is he still alive?'

'Oh yes, he's in his early seventies, has just completed a law degree and is about to finish another book.'

'Sounds like a man who aims to get the most out of his life. What of your mother, brothers and sisters?'

Willard skilfully summarised his family history, but when he mentioned Walter's death at Passchendaele, he noticed Lloyd George's agitation. He had been prime minister at the time of the battle.

'I am sorry about your brother, Willard. It was an ill-advised offensive, one that I was sceptical about. But the War Cabinet supported General Haig and that was it.'

Willard felt he may have inadvertently embarrassed Lloyd George and tried to change tack. He had noticed an impressive picture hanging over the mantelpiece, by an artist he recognised.

'Is that a Frank Brangwen picture?'

'You know him?' David Matthews asked. 'Where on earth have you come across a Brangwen before? Lloyd George and I are great admirers of his work, but he is not everyone's cup of tea.'

'My father was just about to start his law degree when the new Manitoba Legislative Building was finished in Winnipeg in 1920, and he took Evelyn and me to see it. We were standing in the rotunda, a marble antechamber waiting for the tour guide to lead us into the assembly chamber, when we looked up. There it was, a huge, stunning mural by Frank Brangwen depicting World War One. In the centre of the painting is a man tattered in rags, his left chest and arm exposed, being helped along by a fellow soldier. And above the man is a depiction of the Madonna and Child. My father was visibly moved by the mural and asked a number of questions about the artist. Once he gets his teeth into something, he tends to follow it up, and he ended up researching Brangwen's story thoroughly. Anglo-Welsh parentage, self-taught, didn't follow anyone's style. An artistic maverick if you like. What is this one called?'

'*The Buccaneers*. It's oil on canvas, and is only a print, but I agree with everything you say, Willard. Brangwen painted it when he was only twenty-five, which I find extraordinary. Fascinating, too, that there is that connection with Winnipeg. I had no idea.'

'And pray tell me,' Willard said, indicating two

framed Welsh sayings on either side of the painting. 'My father is a keen student of language. He would love to know what these mean. Can you enlighten me, Mr Matthews?'

'We don't stand on ceremony in this house, Willard. Both Lloyd George and I are lads with provincial upbringings. We decry the class system, and we are believers in a meritocracy. What I mean, in my convoluted way, is call me David! The phrase on the left reads, "*Cenedl heb iaith, cenedl heb galon*". "A nation without language is a nation without heart". The other one, "*Benthyg dros amser byr yw popeth a geir yn y byd hwn*", means "Everything you have in this world is just borrowed for a short time." '

Willard savoured the lyrical pronunciation of his host as he mulled over the phrases' meanings.

'Have they struck a chord with you?' asked David Matthews.

'It's almost uncanny. I have told you of my adopted brother, George Maclean.' The listening men nodded. 'Well, he espouses exactly those sentiments. His people are proud of their identity, resisting pressure to behave as the white man. Part of that identity is embroiled with their language, and they fiercely defend it. You see, they believe the white man is scalping the land, leaving no resources for his descendants. He would be very interested to see that your tribe and his are of the same mind. That is, if you don't mind me calling the Welsh a tribe?'

'Not at all,' answered Lloyd George. 'For that is what we are. The Scots have their clans, and we Welsh have a tribal responsibility to ensure we respect our traditions and yet move forward with the times. Your adopted brother sounds like another interesting man, and I have sympathy for his cause. Tell me, Willard, where do you stand on the subject of dominion autonomy in foreign trade?'

'I assume you mean in relation to Canada?' asked Willard.

'I do.'

Lloyd George was testing the young doctor out. The Chanak Crisis of 1922 had led to his resignation as prime minister. During the crisis, Lloyd George threatened to declare war against Turkey on behalf of the UK and the Dominions. But he had not consulted the Dominions, and the Canadian government disavowed the ultimatum, saying that it alone had the authority to declare war on behalf of Canada. The other Dominion prime ministers followed Canada's lead, leading to a loss of confidence in Lloyd George.

Willard wondered what to do. Should he sit on the fence and give a guarded response, or say what he really thought? He plumped for the latter. He believed in Canada's autonomy, and valued the links his country had with the UK, but he agreed wholeheartedly that the Dominions should ultimately become independent.

David Matthews smiled. Lloyd George smiled. The silence stretched. Had he said something to offend? What Willard didn't know was that in 1921 David Matthews had tabled a Bill in the House of Commons to create a Secretary of State for Wales. Lloyd George had not supported it. A year later, during the Chanak Crisis, David Matthews had accused Lloyd George of duplicitous behaviour: the prime minister had argued for devolved power for Wales but was now advocating the opposite for the Dominons. It had been a bone of contention between the two friends.

Lloyd George finally broke the silence with a laugh. 'I was wrong! I was wrong. I admit it, David. Everybody makes mistakes, it's just that mine, in this instance were very costly. And I appreciate your honesty, Willard. Interestingly, in the autumn of this year, there is to be an Imperial Conference in London, where I am sure we will move away from the concept of a centralised British Empire in favour of a more decentralised Commonwealth. Once that process has started, what you wish for, Willard, is sure to materialise. It's just a question of when.'

The former prime minister broke off as Enid knocked on the door, politely informing the gentlemen it was time for dinner.

The die was cast. As they ate, Enid watched her shy but genial Canadian engage with her father and his esteemed guest and hold his own. Willard was not a man of bluff and bluster; he was straightforward and honest, able to talk about art and politics without seeming vacuous or pretentious. What is more, she knew her father liked him. That was half the battle, possibly more than that. Regardless of the whys and wherefores, the courtship had begun.

However, Willard had a notion that anyone serious about their work should not get married until the age of thirty, and he stayed true to that philosophy, only proposing to Enid when he'd reached that age in the summer of 1929. After accepting his proposal, Enid whispered to her new fiancé, 'About time too.'

In the intervening period, Willard had worked tirelessly to establish himself. As a general surgeon in Swansea, he had been involved in orthopaedics, urology, gynaecology and more. His brief took him north to Brecon and west beyond Carmarthen, a large area for an ambitious medic to cover. Transporting patients was difficult, and with the help of a local General Practitioner acting as his anaesthetist, he would sometimes have to perform emergency operations on the kitchen table.

He got his Primary Fellowship of the Royal College of Surgeons (FRCS) in 1926, and in 1928 his final FRCS. At twenty-nine, he was relatively young to take his Fellowship, but his assiduous revision was paying off. He had written to his father to keep him up to date with his career, and John was delighted at the progress his son was making.

Willard had a week to go before his exams, and he felt confident and well prepared. He was staying in lodgings in the centre of Edinburgh, where his food was provided and his washing done, allowing him to concentrate on his studies. A gentleman, Mr Andrews, who serviced the rooms had fought in the war, and once he found out Willard had lost his brother at Passchendaele, nothing was too much trouble. He went out of his way to ensure everything was as it should be.

Willard would generally go to the library in the morning after breakfast, returning to his rooms in the afternoon before eating a hearty meal in the early evening. But on one particular Monday, as Willard returned from the library, he found Mr Andrews standing to attention, almost on sentry duty, outside of his door. He would not make eye contact as Willard approached. A sense of foreboding came over the young medic, and his step slowed.

Finally Mr Andrews turned his gaze towards the doctor. 'It's your father, laddie…'

The telegram was from Willard's sister Evelyn, explaining that on the Saturday evening, whilst reading at his desk, their father had suffered a heart attack and died. There had been no prior warning, and he would not have suffered. Evelyn and her husband, who lived in Winnipeg, were supporting Annie, and she was as stoic as ever.

Mr Andrews sat opposite Willard and encouraged him to talk, which he did solidly for the next hour. He spoke with great pride about his father's childhood in Glasgow and about his struggle to break the cycle of poverty and alcoholism. About his moral strength in fulfilling a dream to travel and become a missionary. About his good fortune in marrying the right woman and their adventure together, trying to do the right thing for people in need of help. And most of all about his devotion to duty, to self-improvement, and to God.

Mr Andrews pulled a rather large hip flask from his breast pocket. Willard explained how his father would not have approved, but with Mr Andrews' encouragement, the two polished off the whiskey in no time at all. It was Willard's only indulgence of the week, for the next morning he knuckled down, determined to honour the Reverend Doctor John Maclean by getting his Fellowship.

W.G. had always seen his parents as guiding lights,

a constant positive force, with unwavering belief in him and constant encouragement for him to achieve what they thought he was capable of. Willard now felt ready to make his own mark professionally, and he was looking forward to his marriage with Enid in the hope it would be as successful and happy as his parent's union, albeit with less children.

Evelyn wrote regularly, never forgetting to send Canadian fudge to remind him of home at Christmas, and detailing her mother's charitable involvements, which were now her raison d'être. This went on for a decade after John's death, until finally Annie succumbed to pneumonia just before the outbreak of the Second World War.

When he received the news, Willard reflected on her life, which had been characterised by service and devotion to cause, whether it was her husband's, the Blood's or her own family's. She was as selfless a person as one could hope to meet, but could also be as feisty as a cornered raccoon when she needed to be. He often thought of the example set by his parents. He and Enid now had two boys, John being born in 1931 and David in 1933, although in 1939, just as Annie passed away, Enid was readying her boys for evacuation to the countryside, away from the dangers of the Blitz.

In 1975, Willard, president of the Welsh Surgical Society and youngest child of the Reverend Doctor John Maclean, died, though not before he had told his sons and grandchildren enough stories about Canada and his family there to catch their imaginations. It was his elder son, also called John, who took on the mantel of researcher and family archivist.

Before WG died he gave John all of the letters and documents he had from his father, entrusting them to his safe-keeping. The majority of the reverend doctor's huge collection of books and papers had been donated by Evelyn to the public archives of Canada in Ottawa and to the United Church Archives in Toronto. John resolved to make the journey to see them. Apart from anything else, he wanted to know more about his Uncle George, who had died at the ripe old age of ninety-six on Boxing Day 1967.

In 1985, he did indeed make the pilgrimage out to Canada. In Toronto, he and his family met Arni Brownstone, an archivist and curator at the Royal Ontario Museum, who was able to show them some of the reverend doctor's artefacts. They then went up to Winnipeg, where Maclean Mission was still operating, before travelling around Alberta down to the Calgary area. They drove out to Fort Macleod and the Stoney Reservation.

There, John introduced himself to his cousin Bill, who was overjoyed to meet him. He took John to George's grave, where there was a cross which said:

'TATANGA MANI – CHIEF WALKING BUFFALO
Gone to the Happy Hunting Grounds
GEORGE MACLEAN – Life's Work Well Done'

John explained that he knew much about Walking Buffalo up until the time Willard had left Canada, but very little since then.

'Let us eat, and I will tell you all about it,' said Bill.

Chapter Seventeen

When Moses Bearspaw died in nineteen twenty, my dad, Minor Chief Walking Buffalo, became head chief. He was a good talker but also a good listener, and he was popular with his own people and with white folk, who all called him "George Maclean".

' "Chief" wasn't just an honorary title. My father and his councillors had to make decisions about capital investments from the tribe's trust fund, which had built up through the sale of grazing leases, hay, timber, gravel and other resources.

'Times were changing, and Dad was a good diplomat, a man who could broker agreement between whites and indigenous people. He told me that the reverend doctor always argued the best way forward lay in the education of the young. My father agreed, but he was adamant that the schools be on our land.

'His resounding message was that our young people should be searchers for the truth. For him, education was all about that journey. He found it sad that so many educated people had very little understanding of the wonders of the Great Spirit. He wanted our schools to develop the person "as a whole not just someone who passed exams".

'He had become chief at forty-nine, and although he enjoyed the job of representing his people, after fifteen years he felt he had fallen behind in his thinking and his search for the truth. They were difficult times. We were in the Great Depression, with severe unemployment, and my dad, at sixty-four, knew that the tribe needed some fresh blood. He stepped down and was replaced by David Bearspaw, the youngest son of old Jacob.

'My dad spent the summer wandering without a horse, or a tipi, even without food. He roamed, eating when he found something edible, sleeping under spruce trees when he felt the urge. He said nature's great house seemed swept and dusted for his coming. The prairies were over cultivated and barren, but near the mountains, the grass was green and lush. In the soil, on its surface and in the air, life was abundant. He ate fleshy roots and stems of soft plants, mushrooms, dandelion leaves, the inner bark of aspens and green berries. At home my mum didn't worry. She understood his purpose and knew how resourceful he was. He would always return invigorated from these trips. Sometimes they would last days, sometimes weeks, but reconnecting with nature invariably did him good.

'During his time as chief, my dad established some good white friends, one of whom was called Norman Luxton, a trader, publisher, and director of Banff

Indian Days, which were events to celebrate aboriginal culture, sponsored by Banff citizens and Stonies.

'On these days, we would all head into Banff in our regalia, race our horses up and down the main street and conduct powerful powwows. All of this delighted the tourists. One afternoon, during such an event, Norman caught hold of my father and asked a favour of him. A friend of his, Frank Buchman, was to stay in a hotel in town. He was leader of the Oxford Group, latterly known as the Moral Rearmament Movement (now Initiatives of Change.)

"Is he a good man?" Walking Buffalo asked. "Tell me about him."

'Norman explained that Buchman identified the root problems in the world as dishonesty, selfishness and fear. These traits were increasingly prevalent in men, and consequently in nations as a whole, and lead to crime, unemployment, divorce, depression and war. Buchman advocated that spiritual recovery must precede economic recovery. If you wanted an answer for the problems of the world, the best place to start was with yourself. But Buchman always stressed that this process of changing your life was not a matter of technique, so much as the natural result of asking God for direction.

'My father was hooked. This man's philosophy seemed to echo his own.

'Luxton elaborated, telling him that Buchman was always willing to work with people of different religions, without the demand that they convert to Christianity.

His work was based on his philosophy of the "five C's": confidence, confession, conviction, conversion and continuance. Progress would not be made unless the other person had confidence in you. Growth required honesty – confession – both with Buchman and oneself. Conviction of sin underpinned a real desire to change, which in turn would lead to conversion and God's way. Continuance, the most neglected of the C's, meant the ongoing support of people who had decided to change.

'Luxton told my father that such was Buchman's popularity, that his thinking had started to influence the Church. Before he was around, it had felt its job was to teach and preach, not necessarily to find out what was happening in people's souls. But since his teachings had found favour, silence had returned. He helped to show again that the power of silence is the power of God. A cornerstone of his spirituality was the practice of daily "quiet time", during which anyone could search for and receive divine guidance on every aspect of their life.

' "I've heard enough," said my father. "What would you like me to do?"

' "Would you consider making him a blood brother, George?"

'Walking Buffalo grabbed his friend Jacob Two Young Men, so called because he had the strength of a pair of young wrestlers, and jumped on his horse, heading for the Banff Springs Hotel. Wearing his familiar headpiece with buffalo horns, he presented himself at reception and asked for Frank Buchman.

'The receptionist pointed out Buchman, who was

having tea in the lobby. Without announcing themselves, he and Jacob Two Young Men strode in, literally picked him up and carried him outside amid much hullaballoo. He was powerless, but he relaxed when my father whispered in his ear, "Norman sent us."

'By now a crowd had gathered. Walking Buffalo, standing by his horse, proceeded with the induction, speaking in Stoney and English. He placed a beaded buckskin jacket on Buchman's shoulders and wailed his new name: "Ao-Zan-Zan-Tonga", meaning "Great Light out of Darkness".

'Afterwards, Buchman and my father sat down for a cup of tea and a chat, after which we didn't see or hear from him for another twenty-four years. He ended up quite a controversial figure, but my father always approved of the wisdom of his words. He was delighted when he received an invitation to Frank's eightieth birthday on Mackinac Island in Lake Michigan, the American home of the Moral Rearmament Movement.

'It was quite the party, lasting a whole week! The multi-racial integration on the island fascinated my dad. It was there that he watched the first showing of a play, *The Crowning Experience*, the story of Mary McLeod Bethune, a negro educator who supported the Moral Rearmament Movement. He was captivated by the production and wanted to know more about this extraordinary woman.

'The fifteenth of seventeen children, most of them born into slavery, at a young age, Bethune decided to get educated, seeing it as the only way to improve herself. With the help of benefactors, she attended college, and ended up starting a school in Florida for African American girls. She wanted to demonstrate what educated African Americans could do, and she herself exemplified the ideal, going on to become a humanitarian and civil rights activist and an advisor to President Franklin D. Roosevelt. All of this appealed to my father, especially what she wrote in her last Will and Testament:

' "I leave you love. I leave you hope. I leave you the challenge of developing confidence in one another. I leave you a thirst for education. I leave you a respect for the use of power. I leave you faith. I leave you racial dignity. I leave you a desire to live harmoniously with your fellow men. I leave you a responsibility to our younger people."

'My dad could not have written it better himself. He was inspired by Bethune's story, and when in a subsequent performance of the play, the director asked for volunteers of various nations to appear in a number of group scenes, he stepped forward immediately. He looked impressive in his ceremonial buffalo horned headdress and beaded buckskin suit, and when asked to speak a few lines, his soft, mellifluous voice carried well.

'Frank Buchman encouraged my dad to travel to the National Theatre in Washington for the play's opening three weeks later. Don't forget, Walking Buffalo was eighty seven at the time. But typically, he saw the trip as one big adventure. Rather than heading home from Mackinac Island, he carried on to the capital, where he appeared in the play again.

At the end, he was introduced to the audience, which included congressmen, government officials and diplomats. He received a standing ovation. Never before had my old man experienced anything like it.

'From Washington, he took his first flight on an aeroplane. He said he felt like a Canadian goose migrating from its winter home in the south to its summer home in the north! Perhaps this flight inspired the name of his new grandson, who was christened Flying Buffalo. After his birth, once again Walking Buffalo went off into the woods for guidance from the Great Spirit. He returned filled with exultation, determined to play his part in Frank Buchman's movement.

'The enthusiasm was mutual, and a year later my dad set off on a world tour, at the time the most extensive journey ever undertaken by someone of the First Nations. After meeting Prime Minister Diefenbaker in Ottawa, he flew to Glasgow. Imagine that, trying to convince the Scots of his own Celtic heritage as George Maclean!

'He then went south into England, where he'd been invited for a royal audience. He had met Queen Elizabeth II twice before, when she had toured Canada, but he was excited at the thought of going to Buckingham Palace. Unfortunately, the Queen was about to give birth to Prince Andrew, and there was a sudden change of plan. Nevertheless, Walking Buffalo went to the palace for a reception with royal dignitaries and was given a personal tour.

' "Nice tipi," he said.

'Then it was on to Germany, Denmark, Sweden,

Lapland, Italy, Greece, Cyprus and finally Switzerland. Everywhere he went, Dad spoke to groups about his life, spreading the message of peace, tolerance and understanding. After covering 18,000 miles, he returned home physically tired but morally energised. I thought he might take it easy, but after a few months' rest, he was off again to New Zealand, Australia, South Africa, Zimbabwe, Uganda, Italy and Switzerland, clocking up another 42,000 miles.

'He came back home because he was invited to Hollywood, and then Toronto, for the film premieres of *The Crowning Experience*. Now ninety, he then set off for Brazil, where tens of thousands of natives were keen to hear from him. From there, he flew to Europe, taking in a number of countries he'd visited before, in a journey totalling 35,000 miles. At this point he was probably the most photographed and famous aboriginal in the world. But although he enjoyed the limelight, he knew it was time to stop. He came back home, where he was at his happiest, close to nature.

'Your grandfather, the reverend doctor, saw something in my dad. They were undoubtedly spiritually attuned, not to mention philosophically aligned. Each was an ever-present influence on the other's life. Whatever name he went by, George Maclean, Walking Buffalo or Tatanga Mani, his commitment to the message of love and respect for human dignity was steadfast. By all accounts, not only did John Maclean preach the same message, he tried to practise it in his mission. He was one of the few men to listen to us, one of the few men who understood what we were going through.

'My dad died when he was ninety-six, in 1967, Canada's centennial year. There were over six hundred folk at his funeral, and we gave him a good send off. There were telegrams of condolence from all over the world, and his friend Johnny Powderface led the singing of "I'm Going Home to Die No More". What a life he'd led.'

'Fascinating, absolutely fascinating,' replied Uncle John. Much like his grandfather would have done, he had been making notes the whole time. He thanked Bill and his family for entertaining them so well and at such short notice, and headed home with the intention of collating all the materials he had in a book of some sort.

In the spring of 2017, my telephone rang. 'Ruari, would you, Claire and your girls Ribh and Orli like to come to lunch in a few weeks' time? I have a proposal for you now that you're retired from teaching.'

After we had finished lunch, his daughter Emma, her husband Matt and their two children Benjamin and Sofia went for a walk with my family along the River Towy. Uncle John had said he needed some time with me alone. The tumour in his neck was growing, and the only drink palatable to him was Guinness. He poured himself a fresh glass and opened a bottle of claret for me.

For the next three hours, he nursed his stout, topping up the glasses until there was no more in the bottles, recounting his tale.

'You see, Ruari,' he said as he reached the end, 'I'd like you to pull it all together. I know you now have the time, but do you have the inclination?'

Spread over the table were copies of letters, photographs, journal extracts, diaries and the like. I nodded enthusiastically.

'Good, that's settled then. Time to celebrate.'

As he sorted the documents into two large sacks, a memory hit me. 'I haven't told you about Drew's experience at Willard's old hospital, Morriston, have I, John?'

'I don't think you have, Ruari. Go on.'

My son was on his final placement as a house doctor at the hospital and had been explaining a patient's illness to her husband. He guessed the gentleman was in his eighties, and could tell he was itching to ask a question. Drew was concerned.

'Have I explained everything so you understand, Mr Davies? You seem perturbed.'

'It's not that. Your explanation is absolutely fine. But I saw your name tag and just wondered where you were raised.'

'In the Midlands.'

'Oh well, never mind. I just had a wistful notion. A little *hiraeth*.'

'*Hiraeth*?' Drew asked.

'A Welsh word, one of my favourites, meaning a longing for the past to which we cannot return. I saw your name "Maclean" and wondered if it might be a lovely coincidence. But I suppose it's a common family name in Scotland. You see, my mum used to be a scrub nurse in this hospital, for someone she described as "a charming and brilliant surgeon". His name was W.G. Maclean. I've never forgotten it, as my mum used to talk about him all the time. I thought how poignant for one of his relatives to now be treating my wife. It was just a thought.'

Drew smiled.

'My middle name is Willard, and that surgeon was my great grandfather on my paternal side, Willard Gladstone Maclean.'

'Well, I never! But he was a Canadian, right?'

Drew nodded.

'How on earth did a Canadian with a Scottish name end up in a Welsh hospital?'

'It's a good tale actually. Have you got a minute…?'

Annie Maclean

The Reverend Doctor John Maclean

'Mac the Knife', Dr Willard Gladstone Maclean (left)

Willard Maclean with his two sons in 1953: John (centre), and David (left), father to Angus and the author

Standing centre, David Matthews while still an MP. To his right is the prime minister, David Lloyd George

Diana Solomon with the future deputy prime minister Michael Heseltine in 1954, before she became Diana Maclean

David and Diana Maclean in 1959

Dr Angus Maclean (left) captaining the London Hospital to the 1986 United Hospitals Cup

The author, Ruari Maclean, playing rugby for Gloucester

*Tatanga Mani, or Walking Buffalo, or George Maclean
courtesy of Bruno Engler Photography*

Notes

In 1896, for no discernible reason, John changed the spelling of his surname from McLean to Maclean. Tatanga Mani was thus known as George McLean. To avoid confusion the text has employed 'Maclean' throughout.

The photograph of Tatanga Mani was taken by Bruno Engler, a renowned cinematographer. Permission for its use was granted by his daughter Susan Engler Potts. Bruno was a friend of Walking Buffalo, and 'the chief', as he was known, taught Susan to ride a horse when she was young. He also made her a leather jacket, which hung in her wardrobe for many years past the point she had outgrown it.

Resources
J.D.W. Maclean, grandson of the Reverend Doctor John Maclean, passed away in August 2017, aged eighty-six. During his lifetime, he had collected letters, journal extracts and copies of the reverend's personal papers, passed onto him by his father, Willard G. Maclean.

In 1985 he visited Canada with his wife, Ann, and children, Emma and Alex, and spent time at the Royal Ontario Museum in Toronto, where he met Arni Brownstone, Assistant Curator in the Anthropology Section, who helped John with his research.

In May 2017 he passed these reference materials to me in the hope I would write them up. They formed the central core around which the narrative was constructed.

'Jesus, Lover of My Soul'
The hymn 'Jesus Lover of my Soul', of great personal significance to John Maclean, was composed by Charles Wesley (1707-1788), a leader of the early Methodist movement and the younger brother of John Wesley, its founder. Its lyrics are as follows:

Jesus, lover of my soul,
Let me to Thy bosom fly,
While the nearer waters roll,
While the tempest still is high:
Hide me, O my Savior, hide,
Till the storm of life is past;
Safe into the haven guide;
O receive my soul at last.

Other refuge have I none,
Hangs my helpless soul on Thee;
Leave, oh, leave me not alone,
Still support and comfort me.
All my trust on Thee is stayed,
All my help from Thee I bring;
Cover my defenceless head

With the shadow of Thy wing.

Thou, O Christ, art all I want;
More than all in Thee I find;
Raise the fallen, cheer the faint,
Heal the sick and lead the blind.
Just and holy is Thy name,
I am all unrighteousness;
Vile and full of sin I am,
Thou art full of truth and grace.

Plenteous grace with Thee is found,
Grace to cover all my sin;
Let the healing streams abound;
Make and keep me pure within.
Thou of life the fountain art,
Freely let me take of Thee;
Spring Thou up within my heart,
Rise to all eternity.

A Note on the Cover

The silhouettes featured on the cover of this edition are of John Maclean and his adopted son, Tatanga Mani.

Further Reading

Brownstone, Arni, 2008, 'Reverend John Maclean and the Bloods', *American Indian Art Magazine*

MacEwan, Grant, 1969: *Tatanga Mani, Walking Buffalo of the Stonies*, Hurtig Ltd, Edmonton

Nix, James Ernest, 1977: *John Maclean's Mission to the*

Blood Indians 1880-1889, McGill-Queen's University Press, Montreal and Kingston

The Reverend John Maclean's considerable personal library was purchased by the United Church and moved to Victoria University.

In 1969 his personal papers were donated by John's daughter Evelyn to two institutions:

The Public Archives of Canada, Ottawa
The Central Archives of the United Church of Canada, Toronto

His most notable books were:

Lone Land Lights, Toronto, 1882
The Indians of Canada, Toronto, 1889
James Evans, The Inventor of the Cree Syllabic, Toronto, 1890
The Hero of the Saskatchewan, Barrie, Ontario, 1891
Life of Henry B. Steinhauer, Toronto, 1892
Canadian Savage Folk, Toronto, 1896
The Warden of the Plains, Toronto, 1896
The Making of a Christian, Toronto, 1900
Life of William Black, Halifax, 1907
Vanguards of Canada, Toronto, 1918
McDougall of Alberta, Toronto, 1926

He also published numerous pamphlets, devotional books, religious tracts and books published as serials.

Ruari Maclean BA (Hons), M.Ed.

Acknowledgements

Sarah Cairns creatively interpreted my longhand to turn the first draft into something I could work with and start me on my journey. Bruce Jones, Ashley Preston and Mat Beckett provided sound advice, particularly in the early stages.

Arni Brownstowne at the Royal Ontario Museum, Toronto, indulged my family and me by showing us the Reverend Dr John Maclean's artefacts, and cooperated in every way to help me with my research. The United Church Archive, Toronto, opened their considerable vault of files, which helped me corroborate facts and confirm my findings. Elisabeth Matthew and Erin Greeno were especially welcoming.

I really enjoyed the editing process with everyone at Candy Jar Books. Will Rees dealt sensitively but firmly with the narrative, and Shaun Russell provided a clear and concise overview. Claire, my wife, has been an invaluable sounding board throughout, and our daughters, Ribh and Orli, listened to endless tales of their family history with grace and humility beyond their years. My older children, Molly, Drew and

Tadhg, have been equally enthusiastic and encouraging about the whole project. My uncle John's widow, Ann and their children Emma and Alex, have been constantly supportive. The realisation of *A Man in Moccasins* was something dear to his heart.

The final word has to go to my father who throughout the whole project has given unequivocal advice, moral support and, of course, financial assistance. Thanks Dad; thank you all.